THE ALTERNATIVE F1 HISTORY

CONTENTS

POWERHORSE
ENERGY-DRINK
zepter

FOREWORD

The Formula 1 World Championship celebrates its 75th anniversary in 2025. It's been an incredible journey – from amateur drivers and playboys to highly paid professionals.

From the front-engined monsters of the early 1950s and the six-wheelers of the mid-70s to today´s high-tech hybrid cars.

The greatest drivers and the most successful cars have been covered in several books.

But Formula 1 is so much more than facts and figures. I have been fortunate enough to have spent my entire working life in the sport, and I have always been fascinated by the weird and wonderful events behind the scenes. By happenings that don't make headlines but nevertheless are an important part of the history of the sport.

That's how 'The Alternative History of Formula 1' came about: This is a collection of incidents and anecdotes that wouldn't fit into regular news coverage or history books.

Needless to say – it has been great fun assembling these stories and talking to the people involved.

It has not always been easy to illustrate some of the more crazy adventures covered in the book. Some of them are so obscure that no photographs of the actual incident exist. Or happened so quickly that even F1 photographers missed them. That's why some of the stories are accompanied by photos that are more generic and illustrative than strictly factual.

This book would not have been possible without the help of several people. Thanks to publisher Jesper Helmin for believing in the idea, to my mate Joe Saward for correcting my English and to the drivers and team members who shared their stories.

And most of all to my family for letting me live my dream in the crazy, beautiful world of Formula 1

PETER NYGAARD

50's

500 POUNDS STERLING FOR THE WINNER

May 13 1950,
Silverstone (Great Britain)

When the Formula 1 World Championship began at the 1950 British Grand Prix (also called the Grand Prix d'Europe), the prize money for the winning entrant was just £500. Second and third places were worth £300 and £200 respectively. There was prize money for the top 10 finishers, although 10th place was worth only £25. Additionally, the entrant of the car setting the fastest lap received £30.

"A car must be running and have completed at least 60 laps to qualify for an award when the winning car receives the 'end of race' signal," it was noted in the official programme (which cost one shilling). Unless they had an agreement with the team which secured them a slice of the entrant's prize money, the driver's income from the first World Championship Grand Prix was a 'R.A.C. Silverstone Plaque' ("given to all drivers completing the course in accordance with the regulations".) With Alfa Romeo dominating the race and taking the first three positions for Giuseppe Farina, Luigi Fagioli and Reg Parnell and Farina also setting the fastest lap, the Italian team went home from the very first World Championship Grand Prix with the grand sum of £1,030.

SMALL - BUT AHEAD OF ITS TIME

May 21 1950,
Monte Carlo (Monaco)

When the Formula 1 World Championship began with the 1950 British Grand Prix at Silverstone on May 13, all cars had the engine in front of the driver. This same concept was used for most of the 1950s with Stirling Moss in a Cooper taking the first rear-engined Grand Prix win in Argentina in 1958. Jack Brabham won the World Championship in a similar Cooper the following year, and since the early 1960s all Formula 1 cars have had the engine behind the driver. The first driver to take part in a World Championship round in a rear-engined car was American Harry Schell, who entered a Cooper 12 for the 1950 Monaco Grand Prix, which was held only a week after the opening round in Silverstone. With a 1100cc JAP engine, the Cooper was based on a Formula 3 car, but it complied with the F1 regulations. Not surprisingly, Schell was slowest of all in qualifying and his race ended on the first lap when he was involved in a crash with several other cars.

FANGIO RIDING SHOTGUN

August 15 1950, Pescara (Italy)

The Alfa Romeo team with Juan Manuel Fangio and Luigi Fagioli dominated the 1950 non-championship Pescara Grand Prix. With less than half a lap to go – a lap of the Pascara road course was about 25 kms! – Fangio was leading his teammate with a big gap to Louis Rosier (Talbot-Lago) in third place. But then Fagioli's front suspension broke, and the Italian was about to retire. Fangio fell back and drew up alongside his teammate, looked at the damage, and gestured to Fagioli to go on - even with the front wheel resting against the bodywork, Fangio hoped his teammate could make it to the finish. With Fagioli driving slowly and Fangio riding shotgun behind him, the Alfa Romeo drivers proceeded towards a 1-2 win. But behind them, Rosier came up quicker than expected, and with just a few hundred metres to the finish line, Fangio had to speed up to ensure Alfa Romeo won the race.

Rosier passed Fagioli, but the Italian hung on to third place in his crippled car.

ONLY SIX DRIVERS COMPLETE SEASON

September 3 1950, Monza (Italy)

The first Formula 1 World Championship in 1950 consisted of only six European Grands Prix. At the final round in Monza, it became clear that only six drivers had taken part in all six races. The dominant Alfa Romeo team had Giuseppe Farina (who won the title), Juan Manuel Fangio and Luigi Faglioli in all rounds and Frenchmen Louis Rosier and Philippe Etancelin (photo) (both Talbot-Lago) had also done a complete season. Belgian amateur and jazz musician Johnny Claes (also Talbot-Lago) was the sixth driver to take part in all six races. Ferrari drivers Alberto Ascari and Luigi Villoresi only did five of the six races as Enzo Ferrari decided that the starting money offered by the organisers of the opening round in Silverstone was not worth the trip to England.

FOUR DRIVERS OF THE SAME NATIONALITY ON PODIUM

September 3 1950, Monza (Italy)

Three drivers of the same nationality have been on the podium together on several occasions – the last time it happened was in the 1983 San Marino Grand Prix, when Frenchmen Patrick Tambay, Alain Prost and Rene Arnoux finished 1-2-3. But only once have FOUR drivers of the same nationality been on the podium: Giuseppe Farina (Alfa Romeo) won the 1950 Italian Grand Prix, Dorino Sefarini and Alberto Ascari shared the second-placed Ferrari, and Luigi Fagioli (photo) was third in a Alfa Romeo

THE LONGEST BREAK

September 3 1950, Monza (Italy)

When Giuseppe Farina took the chequered flag to win the final round of the 1950 FIA Formula 1 World Championship in Monza, teams and drivers faced a long winter break. It would be 38 weeks – 266 days! – before the 1951 World Championship kicked off with the Swiss Grand Prix at the Bremgarten circuit in Switzerland on May 27. This is the longest break between two seasons, but there were a number of non-championship races (photo) before the Swiss Grand Prix. In 2020, when the COVID-19 pandemic caused the cancellation of the first 10 races, there was 'only' 217 days (31 weeks) between the 2019 Abu Dhabi Grand Prix and the 2020 Austrian Grand Prix on July 5.

TWO WINNERS OF THE LONGEST RACE

July 1 1951,
Reims (France)

The 1951 French Grand Prix at the fast Reims road circuit is the longest Formula 1 race in the history of the World Championship. And it took two drivers to win it! 77 laps of the 7,8 kilometer long circuit made for a total distance of 601.832 km. Juan Manuel Fangio (photo) qualified on pole position, but his Alfa Romeo was hit by magneto troubles early in the race and he made several pit-stops. When his teammate Luigi Fagioli came into the pits to refuel, Fangio took over his car, and went on to win the race - crossing the line after three hours and 22 minutes and two stops for fuel. Officially, the win was shared between Fangio and Fagioli.
The proud Italian was so incensed by having to give his car to Fangio that he never entered another Grand Prix.
While the 1951 French Grand Prix is the longest Formula 1 race in the history of the World Championship, the Indy 500 - a round of the championship from 1950 to 1960 – ran for 500 miles or 805 kilometres.

3M36S OFF POLE POSITION

August 15 1951, Pescara (Italy)

At 25.8 km, the Pescara road circuit was the longest circuit ever used in the Formula 1 World Championship. There was only one such event – in 1957 – but the venue hosted several non-championship races in the 1950s. In one of these, the biggest margin between the fastest and the slowest car on the grid occurred: David Murray (Ferrari 125) on the last row on the grid was 3 minutes and 36 seconds slower than Alberto Ascari (Ferrari 375) (photo) on pole position.

DEBUT IN DISGUISE

September 16 1951, Monza (Italy)

Maurice Trintignant (photo) was the lead driver of the Gordini team in 1950-51. He qualified 12th for the 1951 Italian Grand Prix in Monza but felt unwell on race day. The small Gordini team's starting money was dependent on Trintignant, but team principal Amedee Gordini found a solution. Jean Behra, a young four-time motorcycle champion, had joined the team only a few weeks earlier, but had little experience on four wheels. Wearing Trintignant's distinct helmet, Behra made his way to the grid and actually made a fine start, moving up to seventh place after a few laps. On lap 29, the Gordini engine expired, and Behra retired. He was never credited with his fine effort, and only made his official debut in the Formula 1 World Championship a year later in the Swiss Grand Prix.

FAMILY MATTERS

March 26 1952,
Villecresnes (France)

Family relations were a little complicated when Didier Pironi was born in Villecresnes near Paris in March 1952. His father Louis Dolhem already had another son – with the sister of Didier's mother. In early 1944 Louis and Ilva Dolhem had become the proud parents of a baby boy, who was baptised Jose. And now lively Louis had another boy, this time with Ilva's sister Eliane Pironi.

Jose and Didier grew up in the same neighbourhood and they both became interested in racing. Jose Dolhelm was regarded as something of a playboy, but still raced for several years in Formula 2, and finished fourth in Le Mans 1978. He even took part in three Grands Prix weekends in 1974 for the Surtees team, failing to qualify in France and Italy, but he did qualify for the United States Grand Prix but was withdrawn from the race when his teammate Helmuth Koinigg was killed on lap 9. Didier Pironi was more successful, making his F1 debut in 1978 and winning three Grands Prix for Ligier and Ferrari (photo). He seemed to be on his way to the 1982 World Championship when his F1 career was cut short by an accident during practice for the German Grand Prix. He later took up powerboat racing and he lost his life when he crashed off the Isle of Wight in 1987.
A few months later Jose Dolhem was killed in a private plane crash. The half-brothers/cousins are buried in the same grave in the village of Grimaud, in the south of France.

GENDARMES CAN BE HELPFUL

April 24 1952,
Marseille, (France)

HWM (Hersham & Walton Motors) was a small British team, which focussed on races on the continent in the early 1950s. In 1952, when the World Championship was run for Formula 2 cars, the team entered all seven rounds, and local hero Paul Frere scored a fine fifth place for HWM in the Belgian Grand Prix. Between the World Championship rounds, HWM took part in as many non-championship races as possible, all over Europe. On the way from Pau to the Marseille Grand Prix in April, the team's transporter crashed. The mechanics escaped unhurt and phoned the team's hotel in Marseille. Racing drivers Peter Collins and Lance Macklin drove 200 km to the accident scene in a Ford Consul, and two small pick-ups were found to transport two of the three Formula 2 cars. The third? It was driven to Marseille by chief mechanic Frank Webb. He arrived late at night, and without lights on his car, it was somewhat difficult to find the hotel. Webb stopped to ask a couple of gendarmes for directions, and they not only told him where the hotel was – they push-started the stalled F2 car as well! Not surprisingly, two of the three HWMs retired from the race on Sunday while Collins finished eighth after a difficult race – some 35 laps behind winner Alberto Ascari (Ferrari).

WHEN FORMULA 2 RULED THE WORLD CHAMPIONSHIP

May 18 1952, Bremgarten (Switzerland)

The 1950 and 1951 Formula 1 World Championships were dominated by Alfa Romeo and won by Giuseppe Farina and Juan Manuel Fangio respectively. When the Italian manufacturer announced its withdrawal from Formula 1 in early 1952, it left Ferrari as the only serious F1 team.

Many Grand Prix organisers were nervous that a dominant Ferrari would not attract spectators. A French Formula 2 Championship was announced in January, and one by one other European race organisers switched from Formula 1 rules to Formula 2, attracting big fields and several manufacturers. In early February, only a handful of organisers remained committed to F1 and most of them were running non-championship races in obscure locations. The first of the planned F1 races in 1952 was on the frozen Lake Flaten in Stockholm on February 24. This was cancelled following a mishap with a snowplough, which fell through the ice. Thus the first F1 race of the season, the non-championship Valentino Grand Prix in Turin, only attracted three current F1 cars and a handful of out-dated no-hopers. The writing was on the wall. At short notice, the FIA decided that the World Championship in 1952-53 would be held for F2 cars, with the Swiss Grand Prix on May 18 as the opening race. The change to F2 cars ensured big and varied fields, but it did not prevent a Ferrari walkover: The Scuderia won 14 of the 15 World Championship rounds that year.

ALMOST 35 YEARS AGE DIFFERENCE

July 6 1952, Rouen (France)

The age difference between Peter Collins (age 20) (photo) and Philippe Etancelin (55) in the 1952 French Grand Prix at Rouen was an impressive 34 years and 314 days. Collins, making his third Grand Prix appearance for HWM, started from the third row on the grid and finished sixth. Etancelin, in a Maserati, started his 12th and final Grand Prix from the seventh row and finished eighth. The almost 35 years between Collins and Etancelin is the biggest age difference between two drivers in a World Championship Grand Prix.

THE HIGHEST WINNING NUMBER

August 3 1952,
Nürburgring (Germany)

Car number 1 has – not unsurprisingly – won more races than any other (followed by car number 5). The highest car number to win a race is 101. This was Ferrari driver Alberto Ascari's number in the 1952 German Grand Prix. For some obscure reason, the Automobilclub von Deutschland, which organised the race, decided that all the start numbers would be over 100, with the Ferrari drivers Ascari, Giuseppe Farina and Piero Taruffi given 101, 102 and 103.

TOO MANY, TOO MUCH

January 18 1953, Buenos Aires (Argentina)

Argentina's first World Championship Grand Prix in 1953 attracted an enormous crowd. Contemporary reports claim that more than half a million people attended the race, which saw local hero Juan Manuel Fangio make his comeback after a crash seven months earlier. The Buenos Aires autodrome was not ready for more than 500,000 spectators – and the Argentine crowd was not really prepared for Formula 1. The spectators ignored fences and lined the entire circuit. The drivers refused to start until the crowd had been moved back. But this proved impossible, and the organisers started the race in the vain hope that the crowds would calm down. Instead of moving away from the cars, the fans pressed closer and closer to the track, with some of the most daring spectators trying to touch the cars and using their shirts like bullfighters would – yanking the shirt out of the way of each high-speed 'bull' at the last second. On lap 23 a child ran onto the circuit in front of 1950 World Champion Giuseppe Farina (photo). The Ferrari driver avoided the child, but lost control of his car and slid sideways into the crowd, killing several people. Cooper driver Alan Brown, who was closely behind Farina when the accident happened, later said: "It was like a bomb exploding. Bodies mushroomed into the air, and someone landed on my bonnet, which came off. My visor was knocked off and I was nearly garrotted by my helmet strap. In the ensuing chaos, another child darted onto the track and was hit by a Cooper. The race continued while officials began to stack the bodies next to the circuit. Ambulances were sent to the scene – driving on the track but in the opposite direction to the racing cars. One ambulance driver narrowly avoided a head-on collision with one of the F1 cars by veering into the crowd, killing two more. The police moved in to restore order, and mounted cops tried to force the crowd back with bullwhips. It was reported that the mob pulled one of the officers from his horse and kicked him to death. Official reports say nine people were killed and more than 40 were injured, but local reports claimed that more than 30 people lost their lives on that fateful day in Buenos Aires.

WHAT THE HECK WAS THAT?

May 9 1953, Silverstone (Great Britain)

The non-championship International Trophy race at Silverstone had a strong entry in 1953 with 46 cars entered. Close to 100,000 spectators attended the race. One of them had a nasty shock on lap 9 when the Gordini driver Maurice Trintignant lost a rear wheel in the fast Woodcote Corner. He managed to stop the three-wheeled car safely in front of the grandstand, but the errant wheel struck an earth bank and flew into a spectator area. It flew through the roof of a beer tent and hit a spectator who was enjoying a quiet pint. He was knocked out for a minute or two but came round before the end of the race.

FOUR RACES IN TWO WEEKS

May 16 1953, Dundrod (Northern Ireland)

Ferrari had a busy fortnight in May 1953. The Scuderia with reigning World Champion Alberto Ascari as their lead driver, managed to take part in four Formula 1 races in just two weeks – and won all four of them!

It began with the non-championship Grand Prix de Bordeaux in France on May 3, which Ascari won in front of teammate Luigi Villoresi. Six days later came the non-championship International Trophy race at Silverstone in England, where Ferrari entered local hero Mike Hawthorn (photo), who took a dominant win. While Hawthorn was busy at Silverstone, Ferrari also entered three cars for the non-championship Gran Premio di Napoli in Italy, which Giuseppe Farina won with Villoresi and Ascari fourth and fifth. The following week, Hawthorn and his crew took the ferry across to Northern Ireland for the non-championship Ulster Trophy at the Dundrod circuit on May 16. Needless to say, Hawthorn won the race from pole position. After the Argentine Grand Prix in mid-January, the 1953 World Championship started in earnest in June - and Ferrari won all of the races except the finale in Italy...

ONE YEAR, ONE WINNER

July 5 1953, Reims (France)

When the World Championship was run to Formula 2 rules in 1952-53, Ferrari was dominant and Alberto Ascari was usually in a class of his own in the Maranello team. His first win of 1952 came in the Belgian Grand Prix on May 22 and he went on to win every single World Championship Grand Prix until the same race, held on June 21 1953. This amazing run of Grand Prix victories came to an end at the 1953 French Grand Prix at Reims, where his Ferrari team-mate Mike Hawthorn took the chequered flag.

"HOW DID I END UP HERE?"

May 1954,
Hockenheim (Germany)

In May 1954, Mercedes was busy preparing for its Formula 1 debut, which would take place in the French Grand Prix in early July. During testing at Hockenheim, an oil leak saw Hans Herrmann lose control of the Mercedes at high speed. Unable to make what was then called the 'Stadtkurve', he went off the circuit and found himself in normal traffic. He ended up hitting the wall of a house and being thrown out of the car. Shocked onlookers ran to the wreckage but could not find the driver. It was only when a couple returned to their house, 50 metres from the accident scene, that they found Herrmann lying on their couch. "To this day, I do not know how I ended up in their living room," Herrmann said.

July 14 1954, Silverstone (Great Britain)

When a Grand Prix is stopped before 75% of the race distance has been completed, half points are awarded. This has happened a few times in F1 history. The only female driver ever to score points, Italy's Lella Lombardi, only got half a point for her sixth place in the 1975 Spanish Grand Prix, which was stopped after 29 of the scheduled 75 laps. Seven drivers have actually scored less than half a point. In the 1950s, a point was awarded for fastest lap. In the 1954 British Grand Prix at Silverstone, where lap times were measured in full seconds, Juan-Manuel Fangio (Mercedes), Froilan Gonzalez (Ferrari), Mike Hawthorn (photo) (Ferrari), Alberto Ascari (Maserati), Stirling Moss (Maserati), Onofre Marimon (Maserati) and Jean Behra (Gordini) all set laps of 1m50s during the race. They shared the one point for fastest lap, each getting one seventh – or 0.14.

LOWEST POINT SCORE EVER: 0.14

THE FASTEST DESIGNER

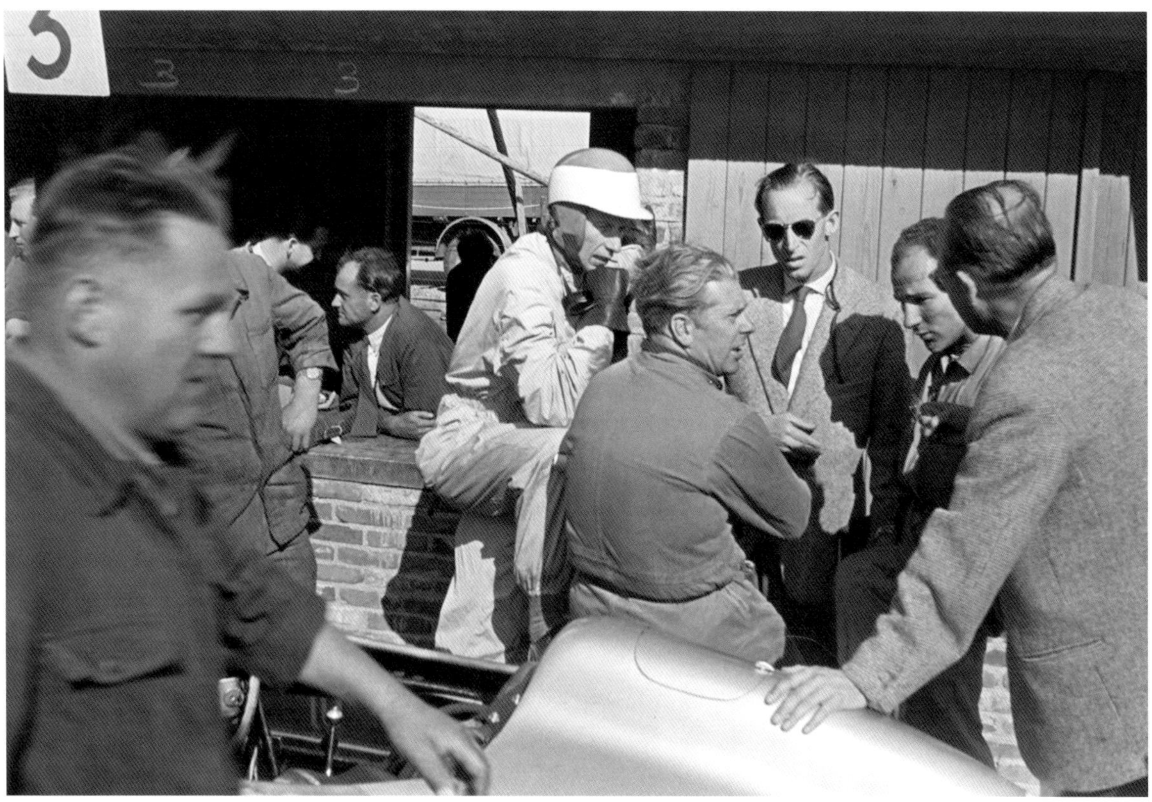

July 31 1954, Nürburgring (Germany)

Mercedes had entered four cars for the 1954 German Grand Prix. But they had five drivers: In addition to Juan Manuel Fangio, Karl Kling, Hans Herrmann and Hermann Lang, a certain Rudolf Uhlenhaut also drove Herrmann's car during practice. Uhlenhaut was the Mercedes team's chief designer, but he did not only develop his ideas on the drawing board – he also tested them in practice.

While he never really wanted to become a racing driver, he was certainly both talented and fast behind the wheel. The designer's appearance in Herrmann's car in practice for the German Grand Prix was just one of many during the 1954 and 1955 seasons. According to the Mercedes archives, during a test at the Nürburgring in 1955, Fangio felt the Mercedes was not quite right. After lunch – a sumptuous affair by all accounts – Uhlenhaut got into the car; still wearing a suit and tie. He then did a lap of the circuit – three seconds faster than Fangio's best time! "He was an extremely competent driver," Fangio's 1955 teammate Stirling Moss said. "You had to be very sure of yourself before you complained that a car was no good, because he would get into it and show you it was perfectly all right!"

CROWD CONTROL

August 1 1954,
Nürburgring (Germany)

It's debatable which Grand Prix attracted the biggest race day crowd. The 2000 United States Grand Prix, the first race at the Indianapolis road course, had some 250,000 spectators and this is the 'official record'. But the 1954 German Grand Prix at the Nürburgring probably had an even bigger crowd. It was impossible to control or count the spectators on the 22.8 km long circuit in the Eifel mountains, but at the time it was suggested that close to 400,000 people attended the race.

While there is a question mark behind the biggest race day crowd, there is no doubt which race(s) had the smallest number of spectators: During the COVID-19 pandemic in 2020-21, 17 Grands Prix were held behind closed doors - with no spectators allowed.

WORLD CHAMPION SWITCHES TEAM DURING THE SEASON

August 22 1954, Bremgarten (Switzerland)

When Mercedes decided to enter the Formula 1 World Championship it quickly signed Juan Manuel Fangio. But the German cars were not ready until the French Grand Prix in July, and Fangio began the season as a Maserati works driver. He won the two first rounds of the World Championship in Argentina and Belgium for Maserati, but then moved to Mercedes – and won his debut race for the German team at the French Grand Prix. He went on to win Mercedes's home race at the Nürburgring, and clinched the title by winning the Swiss Grand Prix at the Bremgarten circuit. It is the only time a World Championship title has been won with two different teams.

TOO HOT TO HANDLE ON YOUR OWN

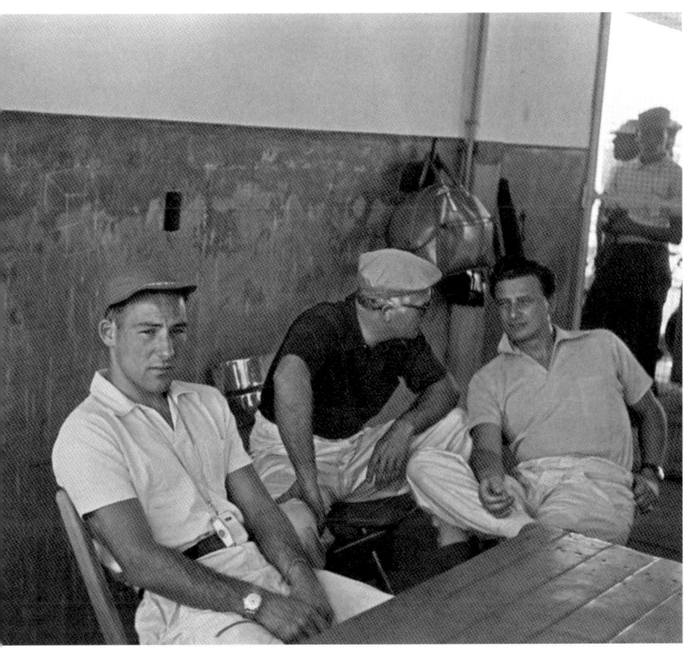

January 16 1955, Buenos Aires (Argentina)

It was extremely hot when the 1955 Formula 1 World Championship kicked off with the Argentina Grand Prix at the Buenos Aires Autodromo on January 16. The heat – 36 degrees C in the shade! - took its toll on both cars and drivers: Many cars retired – and most of the cars that finished had had several drivers behind the wheel. Only two of the cars that made it to the chequered flag had been driven by only one driver - local heroes Juan-Manuel Fangio (winner for Mercedes) and Roberto Mieres (fifth in a Maserati). The cars in second, third, fourth, sixth and seventh place had all had two or three drivers during the three-hour race. The heat was just too much for the Europeans, who made frequent pit-stops for team-mates to take over the car while they recovered and hydrated. In total, there were 16 driver changes. Ferrari's Argentine driver Froilan Gonzalez – nicknamed the Pampas Bull because of his size - started from pole position but had to be relieved by team-mate Giuseppe Farina (who had already handed over his own car to Ferrari's reserve driver Umberto Maglioli). Another Ferrari driver, Frenchman Maurice Trintignant, also drove the Ferrari which finished second, and so Gonzalez, Farina and Trintignant split the six points awarded for second place, getting two points each. Farina, Maglioli and Trintignant also shared the four points for third place, while Mercedes drivers Karl Kling, Stirling Moss and Hans Herrmann (photo) all took turns in the car which finished fourth, each taking one point of the three awarded for fourth place. "I was at the end of my tether," Fangio said after winning the race. "To stop myself from passing out, I tried to imagine I was lost in the snow, and that I had to keep going or I would die of cold. When it was all over, they had to lift me out of the car. They laid me on the floor of the pits and gave me an injection." Sharing cars has been forbidden in Formula 1 since the early 1960s.

31 YEARS BETWEEN TEAM-MATES

May 22 1955, Monte Carlo (Monaco)

The Lancia team entered four cars for the 1955 Monaco Grand Prix for Alberto Ascari, Luigi Villoresi, Eugenio Castelotti (photo) and local veteran Louis Chiron. Chiron was 31 years and 68 days older than Castelotti – the biggest age difference between team-mates in the history of the Formula 1 World Championship. The 24-year-old Castelotti, in only his second Grand Prix, qualified fourth and finished second, while Chiron started his 15th and last Grand Prix from the last row and finished sixth. At 55 years and 292 days Chiron is still the oldest driver to start a Grand Prix.

F1 DEBUT IN SPORTS CAR

July 16 1955, Aintree (Great Britain)

Jack Brabham won three World Championships and remains the first and only man to win the title in a car bearing his own name. But his Grand Prix debut came in a sports car. The Australian arrived in Europe in 1955 and quickly teamed up with John Cooper. Brabham built his own car based on a Cooper 'Bobtail' sports car. He installed a Bristol six-cylinder engine and turned the car – with a fully enveloped body – into a single seater. Cooper entered the single seater sports car for Brabham in the 1955 British Grand Prix. The Australian qualified last, some 27 seconds slower than Stirling Moss (Mercedes) on pole position and retired after 30 laps with engine problems. Brabham's Cooper was the first proper rear-engined car in the Formula 1 World Championship, and four years later, Brabham took the first title for a rear-engined car with a purpose-built Cooper Formula 1 car. He also won the 1960 title for Cooper, and then went on to create his own team. He won the 1966 World Championship in a Brabham with a Repco engine.

WITH A LITTLE HELP FROM MY FRIENDS

July 26 1955, Maranello (Italy)

Lancia was the greatest threat to the all-conquering Mercedes team in 1954-55. It took most of 1954 to make the striking Lancia D50 race-ready, but when it finally made its debut in the last race of the season, the Spanish Grand Prix at Barcelona's Pedralbes circuit, Alberto Ascari qualified the new car on pole position; a full second faster than Juan Manuel Fangio's Mercedes. Lancia challenged Mercedes from the start of the 1955 season, but the company was in financial difficulties, and when Ascari was killed in a freak testing accident in May, it was a huge blow to the team. The Lancia Corse racing department was closed down a few days later, but the Italian automobile federation and FIAT made sure the D50s survived: Ferrari, which was not really in the league of Mercedes and Lancia in 1955, took over the Lancia Corse hardware, and for Enzo Ferrari it must have felt like Christmas: He got Six D50s, 60 crates of spares and financial support from FIAT. The Ferrari team raced the D50 in the latter part of 1955 and for the full 1956 season, when Fangio won the World Championship in the 'Lancia-Ferrari.'

TEAM MANAGER STEPS IN

September 11 1955, Monza (Italy)

Jean Lucas was a moderately successful sports car driver, winning races at Spa-Francorchamps in 1949 and at Monthlery the following year. In 1953 he became team manager for Equipe Gordini, and this job led to a short and unsuccessful Formula 1 career. Gordini had entered Robert Manzon, Jacques Pollet and Hermanos da Silva Ramos for the Italian Grand Prix, but before practice began Manzon had to return to France on urgent family business. Keen not to miss out on the team's starting money, Lucas took over Manzon's car. He qualified last of the 22 cars; almost half a minute slower than Juan-Manuel Fangio's pole position, and he retired after seven laps with engine problems.

MECHANIC STARTS RACE?

January 22 1956, Buenos Aires (Argentina)

Maserati's works team entered six 250F cars for the opening round of the 1956 World Championship, the Argentine Grand Prix at the Autodromo in Buenos Aires. Local hero Juan-Manuel Fangio took pole position for Ferrari and was joined on the front row by team-mates Eugenio Castelotti and Luigi Musso and Jean Behra in the fastest Maserati. Stirling Moss in another Maserati 250F was seventh on the grid. Moss later claimed that it was not Behra who drove the opening laps of the race. He said that Behra (photo) was late arriving at the Autodromo (something to do with a local girl he had met the night before!). According to Moss, Maserati's chief mechanic Guerino Bertocchi (who was also the team's test driver) got into the car shortly before the start and drove the first few laps before he went into the pits and handed over to Behra. Bertocchi's laps are not mentioned in the official results, but with a 4-3-4 layout, Moss was positioned right behind Behra on the grid with a clear view of what was going on. Behra was usually very quick and aggressive immediately after the start, but on that day, his Maserati lost several positions on the first lap. But after a few minutes, lap times improved by several seconds, and Behra's Maserati finished the race in second place behind the Ferrari shared by Fangio and Musso.

JOURNALIST FINISHES SECOND IN WORKS-FERRARI

June 3 1956, Spa-Francorchamps (Germany)

When automotive journalist Paul Frere arrived in Spa-Francorchamps in early June 1956, his only intention was to cover the Belgian Grand Prix from the press grandstand. When he left on Sunday evening he had finished second in the race in a works Ferrari. Frere described himself as an 'amateur who only raced infrequently'. Still, he was gifted enough to take part in both sports car races like Le Mans and a handful of Formula 1 Grands Prix. He was on the grid for his home Grands Prix from 1952 to 1955 and finished a fine fourth in 1955 in a Ferrari. When Luigi Musso broke an arm in a sports car race at the Nürburgring in late May 1956, the Scuderia wanted Frere to stand-in in the Belgian Grand Prix. "I had no desire to take charge of a single-seater after a lapse of a year - and particularly in front of the Belgian public," Frere said. "So I deliberately did not arrive in Francorchamps until the Friday practice had started - and then only to work on my report." But when Frere saw the Ferrari waiting forlornly in the pits, he changed his mind.

"It was the King of the 1956 Grand Prix cars and when practice was almost at an end, I asked to be allowed to try it out - on the strict understanding that I would thereby be under no obligation to drive in the race," he said. "But when I took my place at the controls, there was no more doubt over my participation in the Grand Prix." Frere qualified the Ferrari in a fine eighth place and he drove a magnificent race. Climbing through the field, the 39-year-old journalist finished second to team-mate Peter Collins. "I achieved a success which I do not believe has been equalled by an amateur driver," he said modestly after the race.

DISQUALIFIED FOR BEING DISABLED

August 31 1956,
Monza (Italy)

When he was born in 1927, Archie Scott-Brown was severely disabled, as a result of his mother catching German measles during the pregnancy. His feet twisted almost backwards and he had no right hand, but that didn't stop him racing, and he enjoyed a very successful sportscar career in the 1950s. He also raced in Formula 1 and finished second to Stirling Moss in Silverstone's 1956 non-championship International Trophy (a race which also had Juan-Manuel Fangio, Mike Hawthorn and Peter Collins on the entry list). In July that year Scott-Brown made his World Championship debut with a Connaught in the British Grand Prix at the same circuit. He qualified 10th out of 28 drivers but retired when he lost a wheel after 16 laps. The following month he was entered for the Italian Grand Prix in Monza as Connaught's No 1 driver, but the organisers refused the entry.

That was the end of Archie Scott-Brown's Formula 1 World Championship career, but he continued to take part in non-championship F1 races as well as competing in sports cars. He was fatally injured in a sports car race in Spa-Francorchamps in May 1958.

JAZZ BAND PRODUCED TWO F1 DRIVERS

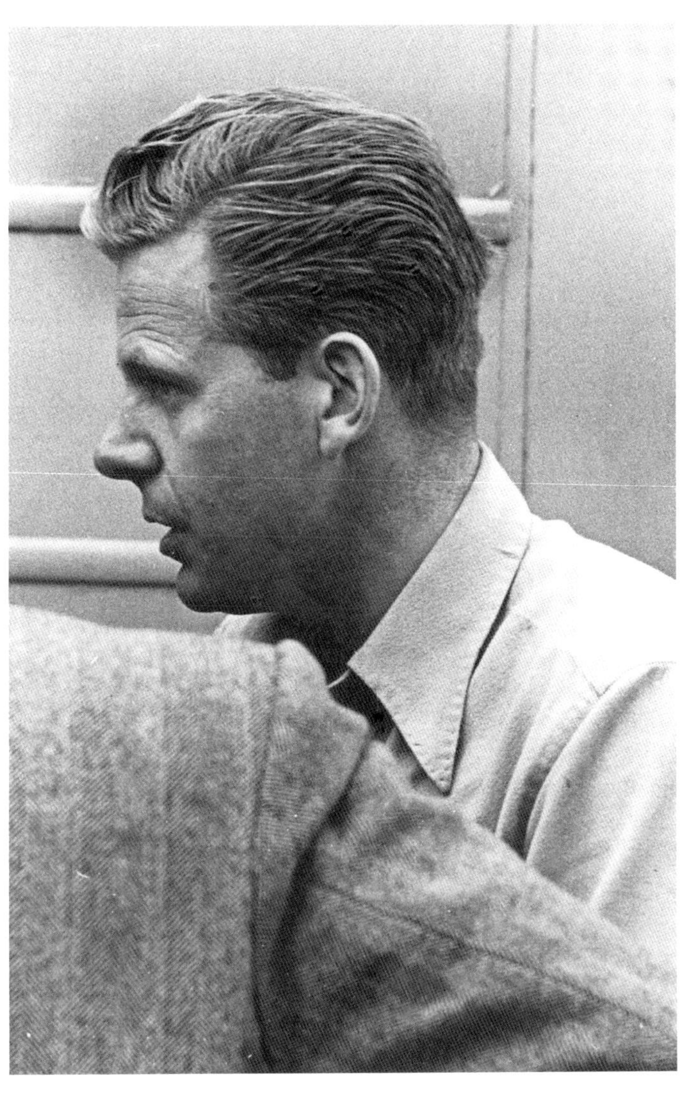

September 2 1956, Monza (Italy)

When Les Leston lined up on the grid for the 1956 Italian Grand Prix, he was the second member of a certain jazz band to take part in the Formula 1 World Championship! Belgium's Johnny Claes (photo), who finished the 1950 British Grand Prix 11th in his Talbot Lago, was a bandleader during World War 2.

The most popular recording of 'Johnny Claes and the Clay Pigeons', I Heard, can be found on Itunes today. It is a little-known fact that 'Johnny Claes and the Clay Pigeons' produced another F1 driver. At one stage, the drummer in the band was a certain Alfred Lazarus Fingleton. After the war - he served as a mid-upper gunner in the RAF - he changed his name to Les Leston and took up racing. He won the 1954 British Formula 3 Championship and took part in two Formula 1 Grands Prix in 1956 and 57.

“GIVE US A PUSH”

September 2 1956, Monza, (Italy):

For 45 of the 50 laps, Stirling Moss (Maserati) (photo) seemed in total control of the 1956 Italian Grand Prix in Monza.

But he didn't know his fuel tank had developed a small leak, and five laps from the end he ran out of fuel in the Lesmo corner. Luigi Piotti, also in a Maserati, came up behind him, and Moss signalled to the Italian to use his car to push his out-of-fuel car. “He did,” Moss said later. “I was waving him on, faster, faster and we got up to 100 km/h or something and then I waved him on so he wouldn't get disqualified: All the pits could see was that I pulled in, presumably under my own steam.” The Maserati mechanics quickly put in a few litres of fuel. Moss rejoined the race in second place, but as the leading Luigi Musso (Ferrari) retired a couple of laps later, the Englishman went on to win the race. Protests that Moss had received illegal ‘outside assistance’ were rejected. “I think it was legal,” Moss said. “The rule said: ‘No outside assistance’. Well, now – is a team member an outsider? A fine point.”

COLLINS HANDS OVER CAR AND TITLE TO TEAM-MATE

September 2 1956, Monza (Italy)

Juan-Manuel Fangio clinched the 1956 World Championship with second place behind Moss in the Italian Grand Prix. But only after his Ferrari team-mate Peter Collins stopped in the pits and handed over his car to the great Argentine. Before the race in Monza, Fangio led the championship with 30 points. His team-mate Collins had 22 points, and with eight points to the winner and one point for fastest lap, the young Englishman could still take the title. Collins's odds improved considerably when Fangio stopped in the pits shortly after half-distance with a broken steering arm. A resigned Fangio sat at the pit counter while the Ferrari mechanics tried to repair the car, and his title hopes seemed gone, when the third Ferrari driver, local hero Luigi Musso, came in for a pit stop. The Italian was not in with a chance of winning the World Championship, but still refused to hand over his car to Fangio. A few laps later Collins came into the pits for a tyre change, and saw Fangio on the pit counter, he ignored his own title chances and in a supreme act of sportsmanship handed his car over to the Argentine. With a pat on the back, Fangio thanked Collins, climbed aboard the Ferrari and went on to finish second, which made him World Champion for the third year in a row. Collins, who had already given his car to Fangio in the opening Grand Prix of the 1956 season in Monaco, was happy to help his 45-year-old team-mate. "I am perfectly happy to wait for another year," the 24-years old Englishman said.

WORLD CHAMPION SIGNS SIX DAYS BEFORE FIRST RACE

January 7 1957, Buenos Aires (Argentina)

Reigning champion Juan-Manuel Fangio took a long time to decide about his 1957 programme. The relationship with his 1956 employer Enzo Ferrari was not an easy one, so another year with the Prancing Horse was not on the agenda. Retirement was one option for the 45-years old Argentine, but when he tested for Maserati in Buenos Aires the week before the opening round of the World Championship, he made up his mind. He signed with the team for which he had won the 1954 title. He had one special condition: Maserati would also have to sign his compatriot Carlos Menditeguy. It did – and Fangio duly won his fifth World Championship title in his last season of racing.

ONLY TWO MAKES ON THE GRID

January 13 1957, Buenos Aires (Argentina)

The grid for the 1957 Argentine Grand Prix on the Autodromo in Buenos Aires featured only three teams with 14 cars, but only two manufacturers. None of the British or French teams made the trip to Argentina, and that left Ferrari (photo) and Maserati as the only makes in the race. Ferrari entered six works cars and Maserati had four cars in the race. The third team, Italian privateer Scuderia Centro Sud, entered three Maseratis. The 14th and final car was a private Ferrari Formula 2 car with local star Alejandro de Tomaso behind the wheel

AN F1 ENGINE BASED ON FIRE PUMP

May 19 1957,
Monte Carlo (Monaco)

After World War II the British Ministry of Defence was looking for more efficient fire-pumps. Coventry Climax built an engine, which fulfilled the new demands for faster flow and lighter weight.

It was called the Feather Weight Pump (FWP) and it quickly attracted interest from the motor racing world. Coventry Climax was convinced to enlarge the engine, and the 1.1-litre Feather Light Automotive (FWA) was born. It was first used at Le Mans 1954 and was later stretched to a 1.5-litre FWB version. This provided the basis for a new FPF version, specifically-designed for Formula 2.

Coventry Climax made its debut in the Formula 1 World Championship in the 1957 Monaco Grand Prix in the back of Jack Brabham's Formula 2 Cooper. The Coventry Climax engine scored its first Grand Prix win when Stirling Moss won the 1958 Argentina Grand Prix in an updated Cooper F2 car. A 2.5-litre FPF engine secured the 1959 and 1960 World Championship titles for Jack Brabham in a Cooper. The FPF got a new lease of life when the F1 rules were changed to 1.5 litre engines in 1961, and it became the most successful engine of the era. The 'fire-pump engine' won 25 of the 47 Grands Prix during the 1.5 litre formula, which ran from 1961 to 1965.

ONE GRAND PRIX, FOUR DIFFERENT CARS

May 19 1957,
Monte Carlo (Monaco)

Peter Collins was contracted to Ferrari in 1957, but when none of the red cars turned up for the first practice session for the Monaco Grand Prix (they had been delayed to 'technical reasons'), he drove several laps in Jack Brabham's Cooper. When Ferrari finally arrived, they had several different cars available, and Collins tried both the Ferrari Dino 156 T-car and a Lancia-Ferrari D50. He started the race in a Lancia-Ferrari 801 – and crashed out of the race with teammate Mike Hawthorn on lap 4.

NEW RACE ADDED AT MIDSEASON

July 1 1957, Paris, (France)

The FIA faced a serious problem in the summer of 1957. Due to the Suez Crisis, the organisers of the Dutch and Belgian Grand Prix both cancelled their rounds of the World Championship. This left a five-week gap between the German Grand Prix in August and the final Grand Prix of the year in Italy on September 8. But a solution was found: On July 1 the FIA headquarters in Paris announced that the Pescara Grand Prix, usually a non-championship race with a rather poor entry, was elevated to full World Championship status. The 25.8 km road circuit in the mountains behind Pescara on Italy's Adriatic coast was the longest track ever used in the World Championship.

It was almost impossible to ensure safety, and stray dogs, goats and donkeys from the many small farms along the circuit proved to be a very real problem. The race was won by Stirling Moss in a Vanwall.

THE (ALMOST) PERFECT RESULT

July 20 1957,
Silverstone (Great Britain)

The 1957 British Grand Prix at Aintree was a great triumph for Britain with eight British drivers in the top eight positions. BUT – Italy's Luigi Musso finished second for Ferrari and Frenchman Maurice Trintignant was classified fourth in another Ferrari. How? Well, British drivers Stirling Moss and Tony Brooks (photo) shared the winning Vanwall, and Peter Collins shared the Trintignant car. The other British drivers in the top eight were Mike Hawthorn (3rd), Roy Salvadori (5th) Bob Gerard (6th), Stuart Lewis-Evans (7th) and Ivor Bueb (8th). There were no other finishers

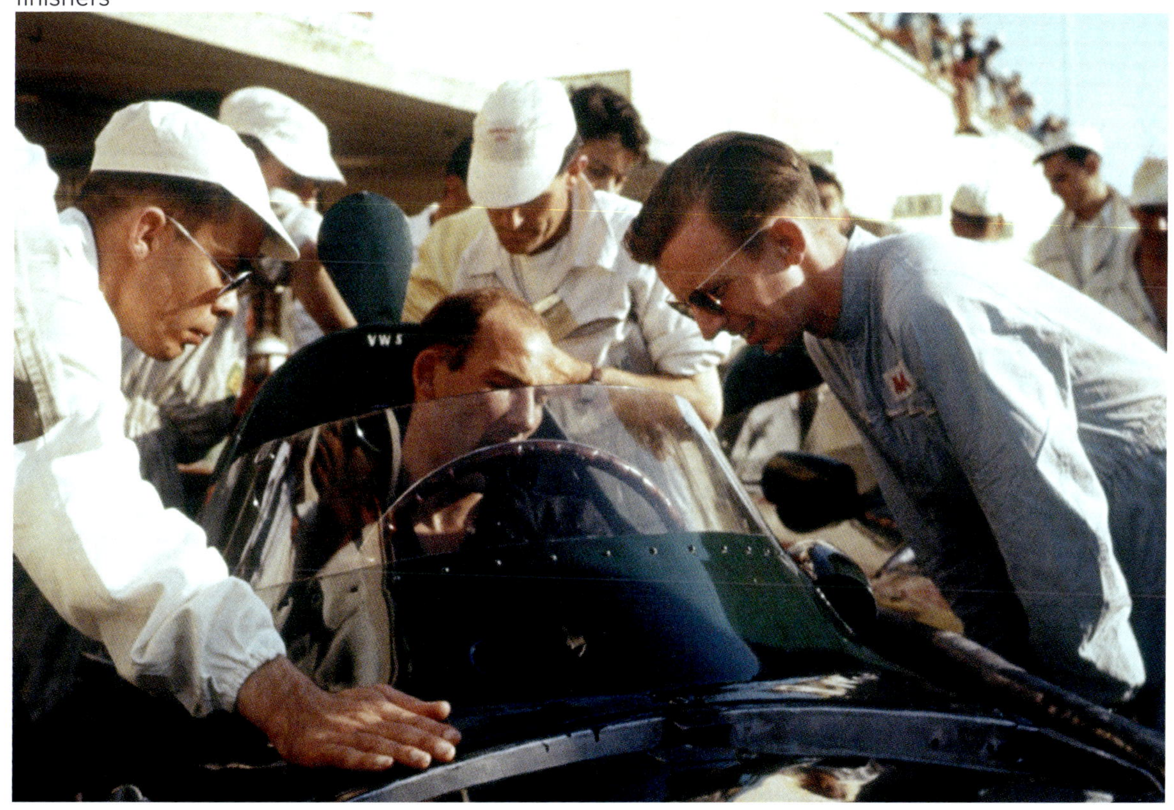

ONLY A FEW LITRES, PLEASE

August 18 1957,
Pescara (Italy)

The Pescara Grand Prix was a late addition to the 1957 World Championship. The 25.838 km road circuit in the mountains around Pescara represented the purest road racing in the history of the Formula 1 World Championship, and to minimize inconvenience on the public roads, the first practice session started at 07.00.

The start and finish of the lap, which took around 10 minutes, was in the centre of Pescara. Out in the countryside, the circuit - bordered by stone walls, hedges, fields and high banks - ran through several villages. On the last lap, Jack Brabham ran out of fuel, but managed to coast into a petrol station. Like all other commercial premises along the circuit, it was closed for the day, but a surprised attendant was there, and he pumped a few litres of fuel into Brabham's Cooper, and the Australian went on to Pescara, where he was classified seventh.

CUNNING PLAN FOR FIRST WIN OF REAR-ENGINED CAR

January 19 1958,
Buenos Aires (Argentina)

Stirling Moss was a Vanwall driver in 1958, but a change in fuel regulations meant that the British team was not ready for the first round of the World Championship, the Argentina Grand Prix in mid-January. Vanwall released Moss to race for another team, and Stirling persuaded Rob Walker Racing to send a Cooper T43 to Buenos Aires. This rear-engined car was originally built for Formula 2, and the Coventry-Climax engine was only a 1.9 litre – 600cc smaller than the front-engined F1 opposition in Argentina. But the Cooper was light and well-balanced and with the race being held in very hot conditions, the Walker team and Moss made a cunning plan: While making noises about tyre wear before the start and faking pit-stop preparations during the race, they fooled the Ferrari and Maserati teams. Despite his tyres disintegrating in the final laps, Moss was able to complete the distance without stopping, and he won the race, finishing 2.7 seconds ahead of Ferrari's Luigi Musso. It was the first win for a rear-engined car, and it heralded a new era. Within a couple of years, all F1 cars had the engine behind the driver.

WORLD CHAMPION KIDNAPPED

February 23 1958, Havanna (Cuba)

Reigning Formula 1 World Champion Juan-Manuel Fangio was ready to go out for dinner the evening before the 1958 Cuba Grand Prix, a sports car race on a street course in Havana. There were policemen in the lobby at the Hotel Lincoln and Cuba's President Batista had assigned a bodyguard for the World Champion as Fangio and the other international drivers in Havana were obvious targets for Fidel Castro's rebels. But the safety measures were not enough. A young man walked into the lobby, approached Fangio, pulled out a gun – and walked off with the World Champion. The rebels were extremely polite: "We are sorry to bother you in this way, but you are the most famous visitor to Cuba, and we need the publicity. You will be released tomorrow after the race," they told Fangio. The kidnapping of the World Champion made headlines around the world, and Fangio was duly released the following day. Less than a year later, Castro's rebels had control over Cuba and formed a new government. Many years later, when Fangio was a Mercedes importer in South America, he went back to Cuba to try to sell the German manufacturer's trucks to the government. It was a big surprise for Fangio to meet one of his kidnappers again. He had become a minister in Castro's government.

FROM 10 TO 31 CARS

May 18 1958, Monte Carlo (Monaco)

The opening round of the 1958 World Championship, the Argentine Grand Prix in Buenos Aires featured only 10 cars, the smallest grid in F1 history up to that point. There were six Maseratis, three Ferraris and Stirling Moss in Rob Walker's private Cooper, which would win the race. For the second round in Monaco, the entry list had 31 drivers fighting to qualify for the 16 places on the grid. 15 drivers - five more than the entire grid at the previous round in Argentina! - did not qualify. Among them: Maria Teresa de Filippis (in her own Maserati) (photo) and a certain Bernard Ecclestone (Connaught). Rob Walker Cooper won again - this time with French veteran Maurice Trintignant behind the wheel.

TOO YOUNG TO RACE, TOO YOUNG TO DIE

June 18 1958, Le Mans (France)

In the late 1950s, nothing was too good, too expensive or too fast for Don Pedro Rodriguez's two sons Pedro and Ricardo. Thanks to his friendship with leading politicians in Mexico City, Don Pedro had become a very wealthy man, and it was time to spend some of the money on Pedro and Ricardo. The boys' passion was wheels and speed. The younger brother Ricardo won the 1952 Mexican bicycling championship for riders aged 10 and under, and a year later, a 13-years old Pedro won the national motor cycling championship in the 125 cc class. Four wheels were next on the agenda, and Ricardo was only 15 when he entered his first car race. Then in June 1958 the Rodriguez brothers – Pedro (18) and Ricardo (16) – were entered in the Le Mans 24 Hour race in a works-supported Ferrari 500 Testa Rossa. The brothers were ready in the pits for first practice on the Wednesday morning when the ACO, which organised the event, decided that 16 years was too young an age for their famous race. Don Pedro was furious but had to accept the decision and a new co-driver was found for Pedro. The following year the Rodriguez brothers were back, and Ricardo was allowed to race, but they retired after five hours. In 1960, Ricardo – by then 18 – became the youngest driver ever on the Le Mans podium when he finished second with Teddy Pilette as his co-driver. By then, Don Pedro had decided that his young son was ready for Formula 1, and he bought Ricardo a seat in the Ferrari team. He made his debut in the 1961 Italian Grand Prix in Monza, and promptly put his Ferrari on the front row. The following year, Ricardo Rodriguez was killed in practice for the non-championship Mexican Grand Prix. He was 19 years old.

BOYS ONLY CLUB

June 1958,
Reims (France)

Italy's Maria Teresa de Filippis was the first woman to take part in the Formula 1 World Championship. She simply bought a factory Maserati 250F (the model with which Juan Manuel Fangio won the previous year's World Championship) and made her debut in the 1958 Belgian Grand Prix at Spa-Francorchamps. She finished 10th and last, two laps down, but averaged close to 200 km/h. When she entered the next round of the World Championship, the French Grand Prix in Reims, she was turned down. The reason given by the organisers: she was a woman. The Reims race director, Raymond 'Toto' Roche called a press conference to explain, and he started by showing a photo of the good-looking de Filippis. "Such a beautiful woman must not cover her face with a helmet and goggles. The only hair cover she should be allowed is at the hairdresser's for a perm," he said. "This is a scandal," de Filippis fired back. "If they accepted my entry in Belgium, I don't see why the French should refuse it. Reims is not faster than Spa-Francorchamps."

She returned to the World Championship for the Portuguese Grand Prix and was on her way to a top-six finish in the Italian Grand Prix when her engine expired a few laps from the finish. Maria Teresa di Filippis retired from racing after her friend Jean Behra was killed in a support race for the German Grand Prix in the summer of 1959.

GAMBLING AND ONE CHANCE TOO MANY

July 6 1958, Reims (France)

Ferrari works driver Luigi Musso was Italy's leading Formula 1 driver in 1958. He had finished second in the season's two opening races in Argentina and Monaco and had won the non-championship F1 race in Syracuse. He was third in the World Championship before the French Grand Prix.

The prize fund in Reims was 10 times bigger than any other race, and therefore it was an important race for Musso. With a win, he could take the lead in the World Championship. And, perhaps more importantly, he could take home the prize money. A gambling habit had seen him lose large sums to casinos, and rumours suggested he was being pressured by heavies overpayment. Enzo Ferrari later revealed that Musso found a piece of paper glued to his car just before the start of the French GP saying: "It is necessary to win. Musso quickly moved into second place behind his team-mate Mike Hawthorn. On lap 10, he was chasing Hawthorn hard – too hard. He ran wide at the exit of the fast Gueux curve, and his Ferrari slid into a ditch and somersaulted at close to 200 km/h. Musso was thrown out of the car and suffered injuries from which he died soon after he arrived at the hospital. The hopes of a big payday for his creditors died with him.

CHEERS, THEN!

July 19 1958,
Silverstone (Great Britain)

The 1958 British Grand Prix was held in very hot conditions in Silverstone. The race lasted more than two hours, and towards the end, second-placed Mike Hawthorn (Ferrari) became very thirsty. Every time he went through the Becketts corner he became even thirstier because some of his mates were working as marshals, and when Hawthorn went past, they greeted him by swigging beers from large pint mugs. On the last lap, Hawthorn signalled to his mates that he would like a drink as well and on the slowing down lap he stopped at Becketts and got a pint. “Then I drove on, sipping the drink,” Hawthorn said later. “I had my helmet off and drove into the pits with the drink. It foxed a lot of people.” Properly hydrated, he went on to win the 1958 World Championship.

TWO FORMULA 1 RACES IN TWO DAYS

July 20 1958, Caen (France)

The 1958 British Grand Prix was held on Saturday July 19. Immediately after the chequered flag, seven of the drivers left Silverstone and headed for the city of Caen in Normandy, France. The BRM team (photo) was particularly busy: Having packed up at Silverstone, their two cars were flown to Caen on Sunday morning. Here - on the Circuit de la Prairie around the city's Hippodrome – the non-championship Caen Grand Prix took place on Sunday July 20. To accommodate the drivers and cars arriving from Silverstone, practice and qualifying took place on Sunday morning with the race late in the afternoon. Stirling Moss, who had started from pole position in Silverstone in a Vanwall, was driving a Cooper-Climax for the Walker Racing Team in France and took another pole position. While he had retired in Silverstone, he dominated the Caen Grand Prix, and won the race a full lap ahead of Maserati privateers Joakim Bonnier and Bruce Halford.

WHERE IS MY CAR?

August 2 1958, Nürburgring (Germany)

Jean Behra took BRM teammate Harry Schell's car out for a few practice laps before the 1958 German Grand Prix at the Nürburgring. Rain had made the track slippery, and the Frenchman lost control and disappeared through the hedge surrounding the circuit in the fast Quiddelbacher Höhe section, a few kilometres from the start.

Behra was uninjured and the car almost undamaged, but the hedge sprung back in place with rubber-like resilience and hid the BRM. With no radio communication, the BRM team was obviously worried when Behra did not return, and Schell went out in Behra's car to look for his teammate. Schell went past the scene without seeing his car, and it took some time and a lot of confusion before recovery operations could begin. The following day, both BRMs retired from the race – Behra with a broken suspension and Schell with brake problems.

LE MANS CAR IN FORMULA 1 GRAND PRIX

August 3 1958, Nürburgring (Germany)

In June 1958 Edgar Barth and Jean Behra took a remarkable third place in the Le Mans 24 Hours sports car race in their small 1.6-litre Porsche RSK. A few weeks later the very same car – now divested of all non-essentials and modified with a central steering wheel and headrest - was on the grid for the German Grand Prix at the Nürburgring with Barth behind the wheel. It was entered in the Formula 2 class, which started at the same time as the Formula 1 cars. Barth qualified the small Porsche 13th fastest overall and ahead of several F1 cars. In the race, the Porsche took a fine sixth place behind Bruce McLaren (Cooper), who won the F2 class with fifth overall.

THAT'S SPORTSMANSHIP

August 24 1958,
Oporto (Portugal)

Mike Hawthorn's Ferrari developed brake problems towards the end of the 1958 Portuguese Grand Prix, on the street circuit in Oporto. Fifteen laps from the end, he made a quick pit stop to have the brakes tightened and lost second place to Jean Behra (BRM). A few laps later Hawthorn (photo - left) was back in second place behind his World Championship rival Stirling Moss (Vanwall) (photo right). On the final lap, Hawthorn spun and stalled. He was trying to restart the car by pushing it in the direction of the circuit, but this was uphill. Moss, having taken the chequered flag, stopped at the scene. "I shouted to him that he would never get it going that way – to push it downhill instead," Moss later said. Hawthorn managed to get the Ferrari going again, and finished second, more than five minutes behind Moss. But after the race, Hawthorn was disqualified for driving in the wrong direction in his attempts to restart his car. Moss then went to race control and testified that Hawthorn had, in fact, not been on the actual circuit but on the pavement when he drove against the traffic. "After all, I was there and you gentlemen weren't," Moss told the officials. They accepted Moss's explanation, and Hawthorn was reinstated in second place. A few weeks later Moss's sportsmanship assumed greater significance: Despite winning the final round of the World Championship in Casablanca (Morocco), he lost the title to Hawthorn by a single point.

A GREAT DEBUT

May 31 1959, Zandvoort (Holland)

Scotland's Innes Ireland made his debut in the Formula 1 World Championship as a Lotus works driver in the 1959 Dutch Grand Prix at Zandvoort. He found the Lotus somewhat difficult to handle in qualifying, and his teammate, the more experienced Graham Hill, drove it for a few laps. The timekeepers never realised that it was Hill and not Ireland in the number 12 Lotus, and when the grid was published, Ireland was ninth on the grid – with a time set by his teammate (who qualified his own car fifth). For obvious reasons, Ireland did not complain. He made a great start and eventually finished his first Grand Prix in a strong fourth place.

FERRARI DRIVER IN PUNCH-UP WITH TEAM PRINCIPAL

July 5 1959, Reims (France)

Ferrari driver Jean Behra was fired from the Ferrari team when he knocked out team manager Romolo Tavoni after the 1959 French Grand Prix in Reims. Behra, who was in his first season with the Scuderia, had qualified fifth for his home Grand Prix, but was delayed at the start. Charging through the field, it was clear he was hard on the Ferrari. At half-distance he was up to third and on lap 28 he equalled the lap record. But the effort had been too much for the Ferrari, and a trail of blue smoke began to emerge from the engine. After 31 of the 50 laps it was all over and Behra had to retire with a holed piston. From the telltale needle on the rev counter, Ferrari team manager Romolo Tavoni could see how Behra had abused the car. Heated words were exchanged, and the discussion continued after the prize-giving. It only finished when Behra felled Tavoni with a single punch. The agitated Frenchman had to be pulled away from the scene by his wife, and he was sacked as soon as Tavoni came round.

THE FOUR TAYLORS

July 18 1959, Aintree (Great Britain)

Taylor, Taylor, Taylor & Taylor sounds like a circus act but was actually a quartet of F1 drivers – none of them related to each other - who all made their debut in the F1 World Championship in the 1959 British Grand Prix: Henry Taylor was in a F2 Cooper-Climax from the Parnell team and finished 11th overall and second in the F2 class. He took fourth in the 1960 French Grand Prix, retired in 1966 and later became the competitions manager at Ford; Michael (Mike) Taylor was also in a F2 Cooper-Climax (entered by the Alan Brown team) but retired from the race. He was badly injured in practice for the 1960 Belgian Grand Prix and never raced again; instead marking a fortune in property speculation; Trevor Taylor was in another F2 Cooper-Climax but did not qualify at Aintree, but later became the most successful of the four Taylors. He was a Lotus works driver from 1961 and partnered the great Jim Clark in 1962-63, taking second place in the 1962 Dutch Grand Prix; and Dennis Taylor (F2 Lotus-Climax) also failed to qualify at Aintree and was killed during the 1962 Formula Junior support race for the Monaco Grand Prix.

BEFORE PRIVATE JETS

1959, somewhere between Brough, England and Maranello, Italy.

When Cliff Allison signed with Ferrari for the 1959 season, Enzo asked him to move to Maranello. But Cliff's wife Mabel, with four young children, said the family should stay in England, and this left the new Ferrari driver with a long trip to work. When he was called to Modena for testing, Cliff Allison had to drive his Austin A35 from his home in Brough in Westmorland, across the Pennine Hills to the Darlington railway station and then take the train down to Kings Cross in London. From here he took the bus to London Airport and a flight to Milan. Another bus ride from the airport to Milano Centrale station was followed by a train to Modena, where a Ferrari employee would take him to the factory by car. "Once I got used to doing the trip, the timing worked out quite well," Allison said. "I could usually get it down to one day."

A GRAND PRIX IN TWO HEATS

August 2 1959,
Berlin (Germany)

In 1959 the German Grand Prix was held at Berlin's AVUS circuit. The track consisted of two extremely fast stretches of Autobahn with a hairpin in one end and a steep banking in the other. The speed was so high – the fastest lap of the race had an average of 240 km/h! – that it was feared tyres would explode, and it was decided to divide the Grand Prix into two heats. Proof that the banking was lethal came in a support race the day before the Grand Prix when popular Frenchman Jean Behra lost control of his Porsche, which flew over the edge and smashed into an old anti-aircraft bunker. Behra was thrown clear of the car and was killed when he hit a flagpole. Only a few weeks earlier, Behra had been fired from the Ferrari F1 team after a scuffle with the team principal Eugenio Tavoni. Another Ferrari driver, Tony Brooks won both heats on Sunday to take the overall win ahead of team-mates Dan Gurney and Phill Hill. The following year the German Grand Prix returned to the Nurburgring and few people missed AVUS. "It was a shocking circuit," 1959 World Champion Jack Brabham confirmed. "Every time you went round the banking, you were glad to get to the other end of it. None of the drivers wanted to go back to AVUS – none of the sane ones, anyway."

THAT'S CHEATING!

December 11 1959, Sebring (United States)

When the starting grid for the 1959 United States Grand Prix was published, most people were surprised to see Harry Schell (in a private Cooper-Climax) on the front row with the third fastest time. His best qualifying time was six seconds faster than his second best, and shortly before the start, he was relegated to the fourth row (where his second fastest lap would have placed him). He protested vociferously, and the time-keepers admitted that they might have made a mistake, and Schell's Cooper was moved back to the front row. This meant that Tony Brooks was put back to the second row – which made Ferrari angry. A report at the time described the scene on the grid a few minutes before the start looking like "a free-fight in a Glasgow dockside pub – but noisier".

Schell kept his front row position but was back in eighth place after the first lap and retired a few laps later. The truth about his sensational qualifying time only came out some time after the race. He had found a shortcut, and without anybody noticing, he by-passed most of the straight and the hairpin, which saved him almost a third of the lap!

PUSH TO THE WORLD CHAMPIONSHIP

December 12 1959, Sebring (United States)

The first United States Grand Prix for Formula 1 cars was held in December 1959 at the Sebring International Raceway in Florida. It was the ninth and final round of the World Championship. Before the race, Jack Brabham (Cooper-Climax - 31 points), Stirling Moss (Walker Cooper-Climax - 25,5) and Tony Brooks (Ferrari – 23) could all win the title. Moss was an early retirement and towards the end, Bruce McLaren was leading ahead of his Cooper teammate Brabham. But on the last lap, Brabham ran out of fuel, and he was passed by Maurice Trintignant (Walker Cooper-Climax) and Brooks. Brabham would only get points for fourth place if he finished the race without assistance, and in the hot sun, he pushed the car uphill for 400 metres to clinch the World Championship.

60's

February 5 1960,
Buenos Aires (Argentina)

THE ARTIFICIAL LEG

Alan Stacey (photo - left) was a Lotus works driver when the 1960 season started with practice for the Argentina Grand Prix in Buenos Aires. Few people knew that the Englishman had lost the lower part of his right leg in a motorcycle accident. His car was adapted to his handicap and it didn't seem to affect his racing. And his fellow-drivers were very supportive: On the track, Stacey was just another competitor – outside of the car, they helped him as much as possible. While he was allowed to race with his tin leg in Great Britain, there were problems at continental races. When the drivers had to pass a medical examination, they made sure Stacey's artificial leg was hidden from the doctor. One of the tests was for reflexes and when the doctor had done Stacey's left leg, one of his colleagues in the room would create a diversion by knocking over a chair or falling down or tripping over – anything to divert the doctor's attention for a couple of seconds. In the confusion, Stacey would quietly cross his legs and wait for the doctor to hit his 'right' leg with his little rubber hammer. According to his Lotus teammate Innes Ireland, "it never failed."

HAVE A DRINK ON ME

February 7 1960,
Buenos Aires (Argentina)

The 1960 Argentine Grand Prix in Buenos Aires was long and hot – it lasted for two hours and 18 minutes and temperatures were high. Local driver Roberto Bonomi, making his only appearance in the Formula 1 World Championship in one of Scuderia Centro Sud's Cooper-Maseratis, found an unusual way to stay cool: he had one of his mechanics stationed in a slow corner with buckets of water, which he then hurled into Bonomi's cockpit at regular intervals. It helped him finish in 11th place; four laps behind winner Bruce McLaren (Cooper-Climax).

TOO MANY ACCIDENTS

June 18 1960, Spa-Francorchamps (Belgium)

The 1960 Belgian Grand Prix weekend started badly. During practice, Stirling Moss's Rob Walker Lotus lost a wheel, and the Englishman crashed heavily. He was thrown out of the car at a speed close to 160 km/h, and he suffered broken ribs, a fractured nose and leg injuries, which would keep him out of racing for several weeks. Privateer Lotus driver Michael (Mike) Taylor arrived at the accident scene, and immediately headed back to the pits to summon an ambulance. A few corners later, the steering-column on Taylor's Lotus broke in two, and the car left the track at high speed. The car went through the trees beside the circuit, leaving damage to the bark almost two metres above the ground. Taylor suffered multiple injuries, which meant he never raced again. He sued Lotus boss Colin Chapman and obtained a substantial out-of-court settlement. He later married Stirling Moss's ex-wife Elaine Barberino. On Sunday, Alan Stacey (Cooper) and Chris Bristow (Lotus) (photo) both crashed fatally in separate accidents.

F1 DRIVERS AT SEA

September 7 1960, Naples (Italy)

The 1960 Summer Olympics took place in Rome, but the sailing competitions were held off the coast of Naples. There were 52 sailors in 26 boats from 26 countries in the Star class, and two of them had raced each other before – in Formula 1. Roberto Mieres, who had taken part in 17 Grands Prix between 1953 and 1955, was skipper in Argentina's boat Mizar and Thailand's Siamese Cat was skippered by Prince Bira (photo) (19 Grands Prix, between 1950 and 1954). It was a close fight between the two ex-F1 drivers with Mieres taking 17th overall and Prince Bira 19th. In Formula 1, the results were similar: Mieres scored a total of 13 point with fourth place as his best result. Prince Bira scored eight points and also had fourth as his best result.

SEVEN YEARS TO RACE

November 20 1960, Riverside (United States)

Los Angeles-based restaurateur, stuntman and amateur driver Robert 'Bob' Drake only took part in one Formula 1 race, but his 13th place in the 1960 United States Grand Prix in Riverside was still significant. When he took the chequered flag in his privately-entered Maserati 250F, it was the end of the road for an iconic car. The 250F made its debut in the Formula 1 World Championship back in 1954 by winning the Argentine Grand Prix with Juan-Manuel Fangio behind the wheel.

Fangio moved to Mercedes at mid-season, but the 250F still played a significant role in his 1954 World Championship. The Maserati was compet-itive in 1955 and 1956 (winning the 1956 Monaco Grand Prix with Stirling Moss) and when Fangio returned to Maserati and the updated 250F in 1957, he won another World Championship title. Maserati withdrew its works team in 1958, but several privateers used the 250F in both 1958 and 1959 – in fact, 60% of the small 10-car field in the 1958 Argentine Grand Prix were in Mase-rati 250Fs. The car was by then outclassed by the new rear-engined cars, but the 250F was still racing in 1960 with Italian privateer Gina Munaron finishing 13th in the opening round in Argentina. That seemed to be the end of the Maserati 250F in the World Championship – until Drake entered and raced his 250F at River-side. This made the Maserati 250F the longest running F1 car – it raced in seven seasons and took part in 46 Grands Prix with both superstars like Fangio and Moss and poor privateers like Munaron and Drake behind the wheel. In total, 26 Maserati 250Fs were built, the car was powered by both a straight-six engine and later a V12, and it won eight Grands Prix and took eight pole positions.

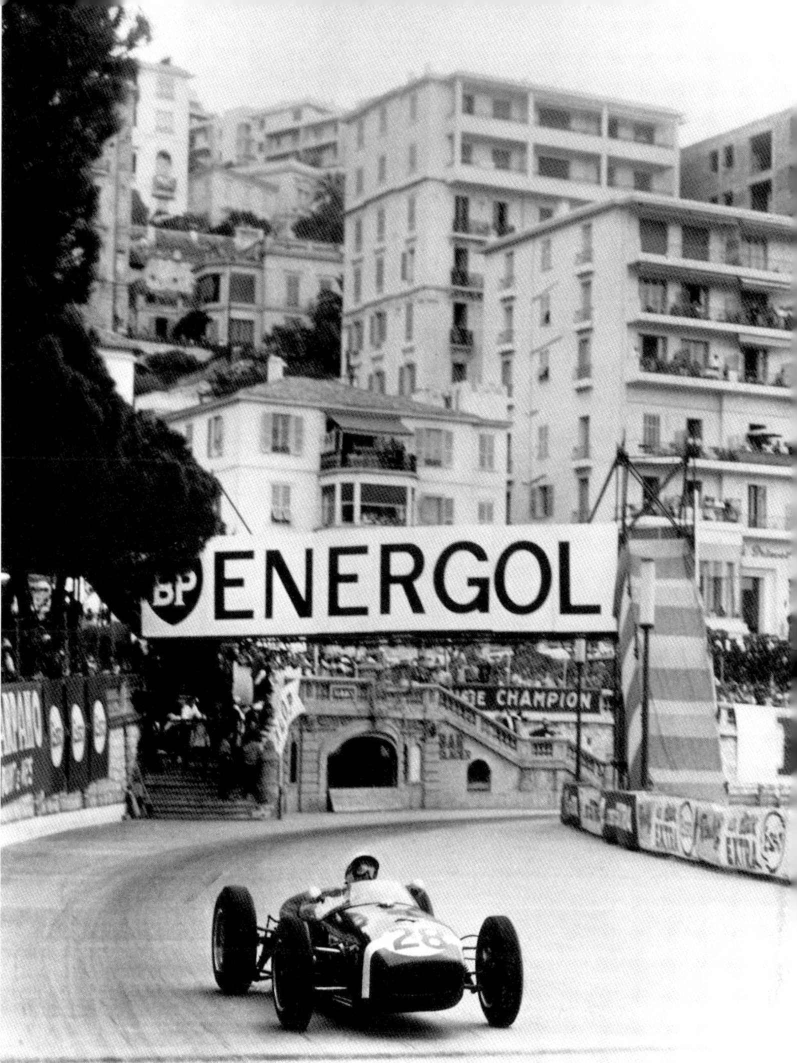

A GREAT PERFORMANCE

May 14 1961,
Monte Carlo (Monaco)

The 1961 Monaco Grand Prix was one of Stirling Moss greatest performances. His Lotus-Climax from Rob Walker's private team was not really expected to be competitive against Ferrari's new 156 'Sharknose', but the Englishman still took pole position with a 1m39.1s. lap; 0.2s faster than Ferrari's Richie Ginther. At the start, Ginther took the lead ahead of Lotus works driver Jim Clark and Moss. After a couple of laps Moss was up into second place, and on lap 20 he took the lead from Ginther. For the rest of the 100-lap race, Moss was under pressure from Ginther and Phil Hill in another Ferrari. Moss responded magnificently to the onslaught of the Prancing Horses. His last 33 laps – that's one third of the race – were all faster than his pole position lap! After two hours and 45 minutes, he crossed the finish line to win the race three seconds in front of Ginther.

BUSY TIMES FOR F1

May 22 1961, Zandvoort (Holland)

The 1.5-litre formula introduced in 1961 made Formula 1 accessible to many teams. And with only eight rounds in the 1961 World Championship, there was room for several non-championship races, and the week between May 14 and May 22 was a particularly busy time.

There were four F1 races within eight days! On Sunday May 14, the World Championship kicked off with the Monaco Grand Prix with Stirling Moss winning in front of Richie Ginther. On the same day, the non-championship Gran Premio di Napoli was won by Giancarlo Baghetti in a semi-works Ferrari. Eight days later, on Whit Monday, the second round of the World Championship was held in Zandvoort (photo), Holland with Ferrari's Wolfgang von Trips first across the finish line. On the same day, Ray Salvadori won the London Trophy F1 race at London's Crystal Palace circuit in a Cooper-Climax from the Parnell team.

F1 CAR KILLS CYCLIST AND MOTORCYCLE RIDER ON PUBLIC ROAD

June 15 1961,
Modena (Italy

Giulio Cabianca was killed in a freak accident during testing at the Aerautodromo di Modena in June 1961. The Italian sports car veteran was testing a Cooper-Ferrari in preparation for the British Grand Prix on June 15 when the throttle apparently struck open. Unable to stop the car, Cabianca first hit a spectator and then went through a gate, which had been left open due to maintenance work. The Aerautodromo was situated near the centre of Modena, and Cabianca went out on to the Via Emilia at high speed. He went across the street and crashed into the wall of a workshop. On its way, the Cooper-Ferrari hit a bicycle, a motorcycle, a minivan and three parked cars. Cabianca, the driver of the mini-van, the biker and the motorcycle driver were all killed, while the spectator hit by the car suffered severe leg injuries but survived. Cabianca (38), who had only recently taken up single-seater racing, had finished fourth in the Italian Grand Prix 1960 in a Scuderia Castelotti Cooper-Ferrari.

June 18 1961, Spa-Francorchamps (Belgium)

Ferrari driver Phil Hill was on his way to becoming the first American World Champion when he arrived for the 1961 Belgian Grand Prix – in a Peugeot 403. Road cars were apparently not on offer from the Scuderia, and Hill had agreed to promote the Peugeot 403. In PR interviews, the Ferrari driver praised the French car: "It's just about the best transportation that I know of," he said. "One thing I like about my 403 is the fact that it comes completely equipped. It has everything except a cigarette lighter – and I have quit smoking."

FERRARI WORLD CHAMPION IN PEUGEOT PR CAMPAIGN

FOUR DRIVERS WITH IDENTICAL TIMES

July 14,
Aintree (Great Britain)

Qualifying for the 1961 British Grand Prix at Aintree was close – very close. At the time, lap times from all four practice sessions counted towards the grid, but with rain on the final practice day (Friday – the race was on Saturday) the second session on Thursday afternoon determined the grid positions. It started at 16.00, and amazingly, the three Ferraris entered for the race all set identical times. Phil Hill (photo) was first to record a lap of 1m58.8s, but this was soon equalled by his teammate Richie Ginther. Towards the end of the session, the third Ferrari driven by Wolfgang von Trips also clocked in at 1m58.8s.

A fourth driver, Sweden's Joakim Bonnier in a Porsche, also had an identical time, and as he had finished his lap before von Trips, he joined Hill and Ginther on the front row of the 3-2-3 grid with the German back on the second row.

ONE RACE, TWO MARQUES

July 15 1961, Aintree (Great Britain)

Stirling Moss started the 1961 British Grand Prix at Aintree in his Rob Walker Lotus-Climax from fifth position. In the rain, he was up to second place behind Wolfgang von Trips Ferrari by lap 10, but fell back with brake problems and retired after 44 laps. But his British Grand Prix was not over: Rob Walker's team had also entered the new 4WD Ferguson (with ABS brakes!) (photo) for Jack Fairman, but he had stopped early in the race with electrical problems. Some oblig-ing photographers push-started him, and he returned to the pits, where the problems were solved. A few laps later Fairman was disqualified for the push-start, but that didn't stop Moss from taking the car out for a handful of laps, where he was actually running faster than the leaders. Cooper's team principal Charles Cooper then lodged a protest because the Ferguson had been disqualified with Fairman behind the wheel and shouldn't return to the race with a new driver. Moss returned to the pits – his race finally over. In the 1950s it was not unusual for drivers to take over a team-mate's car, but Moss's switch from the Walker Lotus to the Ferguson was the only time a driver had driven two different marques in a Grand Prix. Moss's few laps in the Ferguson were also the last ever for a front-en-gined car in the F1 World Championship.

THE STRANGEST CIRCUIT?

August 26 1961, Roskilde Ring (Denmark)

The tiny Roskilde Ring is probably the oddest circuit ever used for a Formula 1 race. It was only 1.4 km long but still had three hairpin bends! In August 1961 a non-championship 'Danish Formula 1 Grand Prix' was held at the Roskilde Ring. Only 11 cars took part, but that was quite sufficient for the short circuit, and the entries included Stirling Moss, John Surtees and Jack Brabham. The 'Danish Grand Prix' was held over three heats with Moss winning on aggregate. A second F1 race was held at the Roskilde Ring the following year (won by Brabham), but that was the end of Formula 1 in Roskilde – at least until Jan and Kevin Magnussen were born in the city, in 1973 and 1992 respectively.

WON F1 RACES FOR SIX DIFFERENT TEAMS

August 27 1961, Roskilde Ring (Denmark)

Stirling Moss wrote history when he crossed the line to win the non-championship 1961 Danish Grand Prix at Roskilde Ring in a Lotus from the UDT Laystall Racing Team (photo - left). Earlier in his career, Moss had won Grands Prix in works cars from Mercedes, Maserati and Vanwall as well as three Grands Prix in privateer cars from the Walker Racing Team. And back in 1956 he had even won a couple of non-championship races in a Maserati entered under his own name. No other driver has won F1 races for so many different teams. Juan Manuel Fangio won Grands Prix for four teams (Alfa Romeo, Maserati, Mercedes, Ferrari) as well as the 1950 non-championship Pau Grand Prix in a privately-entered Maserati. Alain Prost won Grands Prix for four teams (McLaren, Renault, Ferrari, Williams).

YOU PAY TO DRIVE

September 9 1961, Monza (Italy)

The 1961 Italian Grand Prix took place on the combined road course and oval in Monza. In practice, all drivers - among them most of the British drivers - who had not driven on the banked circuit before were obliged to do a special test of six laps at increasing speeds within limits set by the organisers. AND – they were charged 5000 Lire for the test!

TRIUMPH AND TRAGEDY

September 10 1961, Monza (Italy)

Wolfgang von Trips had every reason to expect Sunday September 10 1961 to be a great day. The German Ferrari driver came to Monza for the Italian Grand Prix leading the World Championship by four points ahead of teammate Phil Hill from the United States. On Saturday von Trips took pole position with Hill back in fourth place, almost a full second adrift. With only one more round after the Italian Grand Prix, von Trips could clinch the title in Monza and become the first German World Champion. But von Trips made a slow start and halfway round the second lap he was fighting Jim Clark (Lotus) for fifth place.

Approaching the Parabolica corner the two cars touched, and the Ferrari rode up a 1.5-metre earth bank and flew into the spectator area. Eleven people were killed instantly and four more succumbed to their injuries in the days following the accident. The Ferrari bounced back on to the circuit, where von Trips was thrown out and killed instantly. The race continued, and Phil Hill took the chequered flag. With von Trips dead, Hill clinched the title with one round, his home Grand Prix in Watkins Glen, to go. "I wanted to win. But not at this price," USA's first World Champion said after the race.

HOW TO CLINCH THE TITLE

October 12 1961, Vallelunga (Italy)

For several years, Italy had a national championship for Italian drivers taking part in different categories. In 1961 it was a straight fight between young F1 hopefuls Giancarlo Baghetti (photo) and Lorenzo Bandini, who had both raced occasionally in the Formula 1 World Championship during the season. It looked like a tie, but then Baghetti's team Scuderia Sant Ambroeus had a brilliant idea: they managed to organise a deciding race on the Vallelunga circuit - on a date that Bandini would be busy elsewhere! Still, the ingenious plan almost went wrong. The Ferrari Baghetti had raced with considerable success during the season was suddenly not available, but a solution was found. Scuderia Sant Ambroeus borrowed a Porsche for Baghetti, and he duly won the race against mediocre opposition to clinch the Italian title.

RACING WITH A TIE, BUT WITHOUT SHOES

May 20 1962,
Zandvoort (Holland)

Dutch nobleman Carel Godin de Beaufort was one of the most colourful F1 drivers of the early 1960s. The Porsche privateer often raced with a shirt and tie under his overalls – but never with shoes! Officially the stockinged feet would give him a better feel for the pedals – in reality there was simply no room for his Size 13 shoes (48 in European sizes) in the Porsche!

“HE CAUSED THE CRASH – AND THEN SAVED MY LIFE”

June 17 1962,
Spa-Francorchamps (Belgium)

Trevor Taylor (Lotus-Climax) and Willy Mairesse (Ferrari) were fighting hard over second place in the 1962 Belgian Grand Prix. “It was a real ding-dong,” Taylor would recall later. “The gear-change on the Lotus came out through the back, and he came up with the snout of the Ferrari and inadvertently touched the linkage.” That put the Lotus into neutral, and Taylor lost control. Mairesse, pushing on, came through on the inside, and hit the out-of-control Lotus again. “It saved my life,” Taylor said. “It straightened my car up slightly and I shot down a ditch. If Mairesse hadn't hit me a second time, I would have gone straight into a bank.” Taylor escaped shaken but unhurt while the Ferrari flew, knocked down a telegraph pole and caught fire. Mairesse managed to crawl from under the burning Ferrari, but then spent several weeks in hospital recovering. The accident kept him out of Formula 1 for three months.

BEFORE SPONSORSHIP THERE WAS...BEER

July 21 1962,
Aintree (Great Britain)

In the early 1960s, sponsorship in Formula 1 was restricted to suppliers of tyres, oil and fuel. But that doesn't mean that non-automotive products did not find their way into the sport. The UDT Laystall team (photo) had an arrangement with British brewery Watney's, and always carried a barrel of the popular Red Barrel bitter in their transporter. For those in the know, the back of UDT transporter was a popular meeting place after practice or the race for a few pints. Between the races, the brewery would come down to the team's workshop to take out the empty barrel and put a new one in, ready for the next meeting.

(HOW NOT TO BE A) MOVIE STAR

August 3 1962, Nürburgring (Germany)

Graham Hill (BRM) was on a lap, which should have given him pole position during qualifying for the 1962 German Grand Prix at the Nürburgring. But in the extremely fast Fuchsröhre section – where the BRM was doing close to 225 km/h - he hit trouble. Or rather a full-size 16mm movie camera! Dutchman Carel de Beaufort had mounted the camera on the back of his privateer Porsche, but the mounting broke, and the camera dropped off after a few kilometres, falling into the middle of the road. Hill could not avoid hitting it, which sliced an oil pipe and caused the brand new BRM to crash into a ditch. Cooper driver Tony Maggs arrived a few seconds later, lost control on the oil from the BRM and also crashed into the trees. Both drivers were extremely lucky to escape injury. Hill (photo) actually won the race two days later.

CAN I BORROW YOUR HAT? AND SHOES?

August 5 1962, Nürburgring (Germany)

Heavy rain meant that the start of the 1962 German Grand Prix was delayed for more than an hour. And there was more bad news for Bruce McLaren, when the Cooper driver began his preparations for the race. His entire equipment had been stolen from the paddock area. The New Zealander had to borrow everything – a helmet from his compatriot Tony Shelly and overalls, goggles, visor, gloves and even shoes from other helpful colleagues. It was not the best build-up to a wet race on the Nordschleife at the Nürburgring, but Bruce McLaren still finished the race in a fine fifth place.

FERRARI'S WORLD CHAMPION IN PORSCHE

October 7 1962, Watkins Glen (United States)

Phil Hill, reigning World Champion for Ferrari, was driving a Porsche during practice for the 1962 United States Grand Prix. Ferrari did not enter Hill's home race due to what Enzo Ferrari called 'the industrial situation' in Italy. The decision not to take part in the final rounds of the 1962 World Championship came after a difficult season for the Scuderia, and Enzo Ferrari informed his drivers - Hill, Giancarlo Baghetti, Lorenzo Bandini and Ricardo Rodriguez - in an open letter dated September 21. "If you wish, you are at liberty to compete in other marques for this season's remaining races, with the sole proviso that you respect our contracts with Dunlop, Shell, Marchal and Ferodo," Enzo wrote.

When Porsche's Joakim Bonnier was not feeling well before final practice, Phil Hill took over the Swede's car for a few laps. But plans for the Ferrari driver to start the race in the Porsche came to nothing when Bonnier began to feel better. Phil then turned his attention to the BRM team, which was winning the 1962 World Championship with Graham Hill. The British team seemed to have a vacant car because Richie Ginther was about to leave Watkins Glen as his wife was undergoing a difficult birth of the couple's first child. But Graham Hill and Phil Hill (not related) never became team-mates: The complications resolved themselves and Ginther became the father of a boy on the Saturday night. Phil Hill then watched his home Grand Prix from the pits.

RUN FOR YOUR LIFE

November 4 1962, Mexico City (Mexico)

Mexico wanted a World Championship round for 1963 and in preparation a non-championship race was organized on the Autodromo in Mexico City in November 1962. The start proved the Mexican organisers still had a few things to learn: To ensure all drivers on the grid could see the start flag, there were three starters along the grid. The guy at the front stood on the front wheel of pole sitter Jim Clark's Lotus, to see how the field was lining up - when one of the other starters gave the signal. The poor guy on Clark's front wheel leapt off and ran for his life. Amazingly, Clark was not distracted and actually took the lead.

HILL WINS CHAMPIONSHIP, THEN BREAKS BOY'S LEG

December 29 1962, East London (South Africa)

Graham Hill (BRM) clinched the 1962 World Championship in the final round at South Africa's East London circuit, but his triumph was marred by an accident on the slowing-down lap after the race: "The South Africans poured onto the track and I had to drive round the circuit very slowly in the car to receive their acclaim," Hill said later. "I did not know it at the time, but during my run round I ran over the leg of a small boy and broke it – he got pushed under the back wheel by the crowd and the wheel went over his leg. It was very unfortunate and it upset me quite a bit."

NEW WORLD CHAMPION CELEBRATES IN JAIL

January 1 1963, Karachi (Pakistan)

Immediately after clinching the 1962 World Championship in South Africa, Graham Hill was on his way to New Zealand for a non-championship race, due to be held on January 5. After a stop-over in Nairobi, Hill and Innes Ireland arrived in Karachi, where they were supposed to catch a BOAC plane to Sydney, Australia. The plane was late, and when the Pakistani officials discovered that Hill and Ireland did not have yellow fever certificates, the F1 drivers were promptly marched off to prison to wait for the BOAC flight. "The jail had bars everywhere and soldiers walking around outside with fixed bayonets," Hill said later. "We ordered up a bottle of brandy, which we polished off pretty quickly – and then ordered up another one. We spent the whole of New Year's Day in this way, but eventually the plane arrived, and we got to Australia."

WHERE DID YOU COME FROM?

June 7 1963,
Spa-Francorchamps (Belgium)

The new ATS (Automobili Turismo e Sport) team originally planned to make its debut at the start of the 1963 season, but had to withdraw from both the non-championship International Trophy race at Silverstone and the Monaco Grand Prix in May because the new cars were not ready. The Belgian Grand Prix was next, but ATS was also late for this. The team transporter only arrived in the village of Malmedy when practice was in full swing. That did stop the Italians: they unloaded the cars, Phil Hill and Giancarlo Baghetti got in and somehow made their way onto the road circuit. When the ATS cars got halfway round the track to the pits in Francorchamps, astonished onlookers wondered what they were – and where they came from. Despite the unusual debut, the cars were still not quite ready: the following day Phil Hill in the fastest ATS was some 12 seconds slower than the pole position time.

June 9 1963,
Spa-Francorchamps (Belgium)

Despite winning both the drivers and the Constructors Championship, Ferrari was not a happy team at the end of 1961. Many leading team members felt that Laura Ferrari, the excitable wife of Enzo, had become too powerful, and eventually sporting director Romolo Tavoni, technical director Carlo Chiti and several other key team members presented 'Il Commendatore' with an ultimatum: "Either she leaves us alone – or we go." Not keen on problems with his volatile wife, Enzo assembled a new team while Chiti, Tavoni and Co went off to set up Automobili Turismo Sport (ATS) with financial backing from Italian aristocrats and industrialists. ATS set out to challenge Ferrari on both the road car and racing front, and their first F1 car was ready for the 1963 Belgian Grand Prix. The 1961 World Champion Phil Hill and Italian sensation Giancarlo Baghetti, who had won his very first Grand Prix in 1961, drove for Ferrari in 1962, but joined ATS for its debut season. Both the ATS car and the engine were a disaster, and the team collapsed after a few months. The challenge to Ferrari was over.

NO CHALLENGE TO MR AND MRS FERRARI

THE WEASEL

August 8 1963, Ledburn (Great Britain)

In the early hours of August 8 1963 a Royal Mail train on its way from Glasgow to London was stopped by a gang of 15 robbers near the village of Ledburn in Buckinghamshire. They escaped with £2.6 million – about £40 million today – in what was soon called The Great Train Robbery. Most of the stolen money was never recovered, but the robbers were captured one by one.

One of them was Roy James, known in the criminal world as 'The Weasel'. A somewhat dodgy silversmith with motor racing ambitions, he financed his Formula Junior career in the early 1960s by stealing precious metals and melting them down to create new products. His racing experience made him a popular getaway driver for other criminals, but he was caught a few weeks after The Great Train Robbery. In April 1964 he was sentenced to 30 years in prison, but he was released in 1975. By then he was 40 years old, but he tried to get back into racing and went to see Brabham team owner Bernie Ecclestone, who told him it was too late to make a career. Instead, Ecclestone gave The Weasel the job of creating a trophy, which every year was presented to the season's best Formula 1 promoter. It was never revealed where the silver for the trophy came from!

Roy James died from a heart attack in 1997.

August 18 1963, Enna-Pergusa (Italy)

As soon as Team Lotus drivers Jim Clark and Trevor Taylor (photo) had finished 1-2 in the 1963 non-championship 'Kanonloppet' in Karlskoga, Sweden, they began a different kind of race. The following week, Team Lotus had entered Taylor and Peter Arundell in another non-championship race – at the Enna-Pergusa circuit in Sicily. A few other teams and drivers also made the 2,050-mile trip from central Sweden to central Sicily. This was long before motorways and the bridge between Sweden and Denmark. It was an epic journey in less than a week, and the Team Lotus transporter broke down in Palermo, some 93 miles from Enna-Pergusa. They had to hire a truck for one of the F1 cars, while the other was towed behind the Chevrolet Impala of Dutch privateer Carel de Beaufort, who had also made the long journey from Karlskoga. The Lotus team finally arrived at six in the morning on Saturday and only took part in the final qualifying session, which saw Taylor qualify on the front row. He retired from the race after a high-speed crash. He was thrown out of the car and went head over heels down the track for some 50 metres before he came to rest – unconscious, but in a sitting position. He came around a few minutes later and suffered only serious bruising. His teammate Arundell finished second to John Surtees (Ferrari).

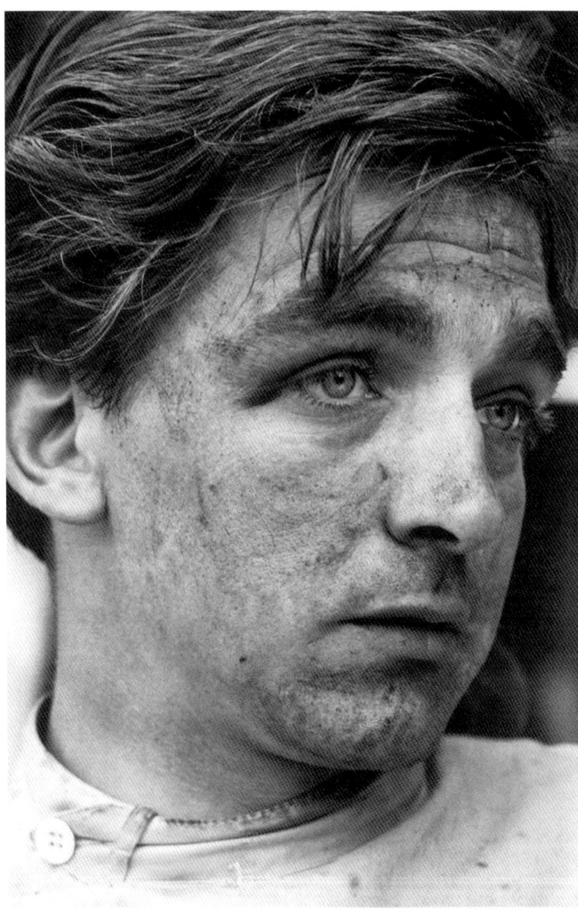

AN EPIC JOURNEY

FERRARI BORROWS A DRIVER FROM PRIVATEER

September 6 1963, Monza (Italy)

Ferrari had a difficult 1963 season, and things went from bad to worse when Willy Mairesse was injured in the German Grand Prix. For its home Grand Prix in Monza, Ferrari was suddenly short of a driver with no obvious choice to partner John Surtees. Before practice began, the team arranged to 'borrow' Lorenzo Bandini (photo) from the privateer Scuderia Centro Sud BRM team. Bandini, who had raced for Ferrari in 1962, retired from the race in Monza, but remained with the Prancing Horse for the rest of his career, which came to a tragic end in the 1967 Monaco Grand Prix.

A NEW TRACK AFTER PRACTICE

September 8 1963, Monza (Italy)

The 1963 Italian Grand Prix was planned to take place on the long version of the Autodromo di Monza, incorporating both the road circuit and the banked oval. When several cars suffered suspension damage on the bumpy 'speed circuit', a deputation of teams and drivers went to the Monza organisers and asked them to revert to the road course. The 'Commissione Provinciale di Vigilanza', the body responsible for public safety at the circuit, also felt that spectators were not sufficiently protected if a car flew over the top of the banking. The organisers closed down the banked section of the circuit, and for the rest of the weekend, used only the road course.

FROM SMALL ACORNS

January 9 1964,
Ockham (Great Britain)

On January 9 1964, Ken Tyrrell registered the Tyrrell Racing Organisation at Companies House. The timber merchant had raced in the 1950s and early 1960s, and even made it into Formula 2, but he realised that he was a better team manager than he was a racing driver. The Tyrrell Racing Organisation – with only two full-time employees - started out in Formula Junior. The team grew and moved into Formula 1 in 1968. With Jackie Stewart behind the wheel, Tyrrell won the World Championship in 1969, 1971 and 1973.
Ken ran the team until 1998, when he was 74 years old, when he sold it to British American Tobacco. The name was changed to British American Racing, and the team ran without much success until 2006, when Honda took it over. The name was changed to Honda GP Ltd, and the works team won a single Grand Prix – Hungary 2006 with Jenson Button – before the Japanese pulled the plug. Instead of shutting the team down, Honda sold the organisation to some of its executives, led by team principal Ross Brawn – for the grand sum of £1!

Brawn Grand Prix Ltd went on to win the 2009 World Championship with Jenson Button, and at the end of the season, Mercedes bought the team for a reported £150 million and created the current Mercedes-Benz Grand Prix Ltd company, which dominated Formula 1 from 2014-20 and today employs close to 1,500 people.

Everything has changed over the years, but one thing remains the same: The company number – 00787446 - which is the same as it was when Tyrrell started the business in 1964.

THESE FUELLISH THINGS

June 14 1964, Spa-Francorchamps (Belgium)

Dan Gurney (Brabham) was in a class of his own in the 1964 Belgian Grand Prix in Spa-Francorchamps. During Friday practice he was a whopping 4.3 seconds faster than John Surtees (Ferrari) in second place and on Saturday he took pole position, a full second faster than Graham Hill (BRM). Gurney also completely dominated the race, shattered the lap record and pulled out a lead of some 40 seconds. Then, with just three laps to the chequered flag, he ran short of fuel. His lead was big enough to make a quick splash-and-dash pit stop and still win the race. But the Brabham team did not have any fuel available! At the time one race report called it "an almost criminal case of bad management", and the team had no option but to send Gurney back out again. He ran out fuel on the last lap and was eventually classified sixth.

CHOSEN BECAUSE HE KNEW NOTHING ABOUT F1

August 2 1964,
Nürburgring (Germany)

Ronnie Bucknum was not the obvious choice to drive the Honda car when the Japanese company made its F1 debut in the 1964 German Grand Prix. In fact, the Japanese chose the American, whose family ran a Honda dealership, because he knew nothing about F1! Honda's logic was as follows: With no international pedigree, Bucknum could test and race the first Honda F1 car with little attention, pressure or expectations. And he would have no preconceived ideas – Bucknum and Honda would learn about F1 together. Bucknum, with a background in US sports car racing, tested the new F1 car intensively in Japan, but the 1964 German Grand Prix was still his first ever single-seater race. He did a good job at the Nürburgring until the car suffered steering failure.

The following year Honda signed the experienced Richie Ginther, but Bucknum stayed with the team and finished fifth in the 1965 Mexican Grand Prix (won by Ginther).

THE SCOT AND THE CACTUS

August 23 1964, Zeltweg (Austria)

The 1964 Austrian Grand Prix was held at a circuit laid out on the airfield at Zeltweg. With many cars breaking down on the desperately bumpy runways, the weekend was a bit of a disaster, but at least the local organisers put on a huge post-race party on Sunday night. Scotsmen Jim Clark and Innes Ireland arrived in kilts, and Ireland had elected to wear nothing underneath. With the local schnaps flowing freely, Ireland decided to dance on the tables. Graham Hill decided to join the fun with a prickly cactus. Ireland and his girlfriend spent the next few days with a pair of tweezers and a magnifying glass, pulling cactus spines from Innes's nether regions.

THE LAST SHARED DRIVE

October 4 1964, Watkins Glen (United States)

In the 1950s drivers often shared cars (and any points scored) during a Grand Prix. From 1958 onwards, 'shared cars' did not score points, but on a few occasions, two drivers still drove the same car in a Grand Prix. The last such 'shared drive' came in the United States Grand Prix in 1964. Team Lotus's reigning World Champion Jim Clark (photo - centre) was still in with a chance of taking a second consecutive title and was running in third and gaining on the leaders when his car began to misfire. He stopped in the pits for repairs and returned to the race, but only for a few laps. Then it was back to the pits, where Lotus boss Colin Chapman (phot - left) called his other driver, Mike Spence (photo - right), in from fourth place. Clark took over the car – he, of course, was not able to score points in Spence's car, but he could still push the other championship contenders down in the points rankings. The great Scot was up to third and gaining on the leaders when he also had to retire the second Lotus a few laps from the end.

WORLD CHAMPIONSHIP CHANGES HANDS TWICE ON LAST LAP

October 25 1964, Mexico City (Mexico)

When the last lap of the final round of the 1964 World Championship began, Jim Clark (Lotus) was on his way to the title, on the Mexico City circuit. Halfway round the lap, Graham Hill (BRM) was briefly World Champion but when the chequered flag came out, the title went to John Surtees (Ferrari) (photo). Before the race in Mexico City, Hill was leading the World Championship with 39 points. Surtees was second with 34 and with nine points to the winner of each race, Clark was only an outsider with 30 points. Hill's race ended when he was hit from behind by Surtees's Ferrari team-mate Lorenzo Bandini. The shunt damaged the BRM's exhaust system and after a couple of pit-stops, Hill could only finish in 11th. Clark had been leading the race from the start and with Hill out of the points and Surtees down in fourth place, the Lotus driver looked destined to take the title. By winning the race, Clark would be equal on points with Hill and would have more race wins. But Clark's engine was losing oil towards the end. He was still leading when he came up to start the final lap, but the engine seized shortly afterwards. With Clark classified fifth and Surtees only up to third, Hill would take the title. Agitated signals from the Ferrari pits made it clear to second-placed Bandini that he should let Surtees pass, so when the chequered flag came out for winner Dan Gurney (Brabham), Surtees was second ahead of his team-mate.

This was enough to make John Surtees the 1964 World Champion. “Bandini certainly earned his money for Ferrari that day,” Graham Hill would say later. “But it was a very good championship season and a very exciting finish. Real Hollywood style.” Despite losing the World Championship in the controversial shunt with Bandini, Hill was convinced that the Italian didn't hit him on purpose. “Of course, he didn't mean to do it. It was just bloody bad driving,” Hill said of Bandini's attack. And a few weeks later Hill sent Bandini a special Christmas present: An LP record entitled ‘Advanced Driving Lessons’.

NO CHAMPAGNE FOR NEW YEAR'S EVE

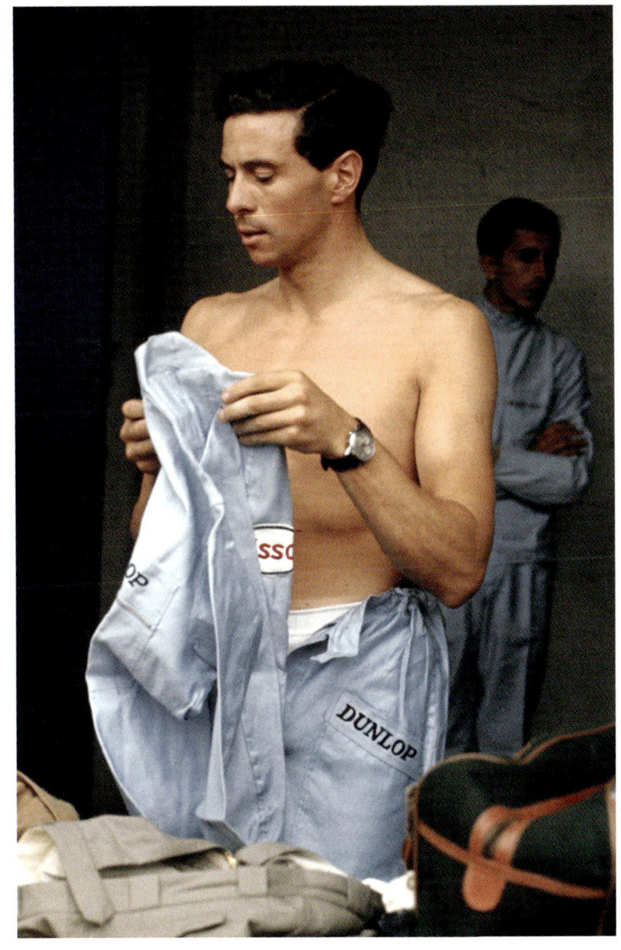

January 1 1965,
Kyalami (South Africa)

The 1965 South African Grand Prix took place on a Friday – but that was not the most unusual thing about the race at the East London circuit: The first round of the 1965 World Championship was run on New Year's Day. Practice and qualifying for the race had been held on December 30 and 31, the previous year! The Formula 1 drivers had a quiet New Year's Eve before the start of the race at 14.00 on New Year's Day. A mistake by the organisers saw winner Jim Clark (photo) being shown the chequered flag one lap too early, but fortunately the Lotus driver had been given a last-lap signal by team principal Jim Clark and he continued to complete the full distance. He then had the unique experience of being flagged twice. Some New Year celebrations!

HILL'S PUSH TO WIN

May 30 1965, Monte Carlo (Monaco)

Graham Hill (BRM) started the 1965 Monaco Grand Prix from pole position and quickly built up a strong lead. After some 25 laps it was time to lap the slow-going privateer Bob Anderson (Brabham) before the chicane - but it all went wrong. "All I could see as I blasted over the hill was that he was going to be occupying the chicane at about the time that I wanted to flash through it," Hill explained later. His only option was to go straight down the escape road and then brake hard. "I came to a grinding halt well up the escape road," he went on. "I had to get out of the car, push it backwards onto the track, climb in and then start the engine. I lost about 35 seconds." Hill then started a great comeback, and at the end of the 100-lap race he was back in the lead, winning his third Monaco Grand Prix in a row.

HAWKINS GOES SWIMMING DURING MONACO GRAND PRIX

May 30 1965, Monte Carlo (Monaco)

Australian Lotus privateer Paul Hawkins survived a trip to the bottom of the Monte Carlo harbour during the 1965 Monaco Grand Prix. Hawkins lost control of his Lotus on the 79th of 100 laps. He slid backwards through the chicane and finished up in the harbour. Hawkins, an excellent swimmer, stayed in the car until it settled on the bottom, about 10 metres down. After Alberto Ascari (Lancia) had survived a plunge into the Monte Carlo harbour in 1955, frogmen had always been on standby in the harbour area, and one of them quickly reached Hawkins. The ultra-cool Australian grabbed the mouthpiece from his saviour, took several deep breaths and shot to the surface – followed by a somewhat spluttering frogman.

STARTING MONEY: £20

June 11 1965,
Spa-Francorchamps (Belgium)

The first practice day for the 1965 Belgian Grand Prix was marked by discussions about starting money. A deal was already in place with the five works teams from Ferrari, Lotus, BRM, Cooper and Honda, but the privateers were not happy. The Belgian organisers only offered serious starting money to the four fastest privateers in qualifying – the remaining five would only receive £20 each (equivalent to about $100 today). Eventually, a compromise was agreed, but clearly life as a privateer Formula 1 driver in the mid-1960s was neither lucrative nor glamorous.

TAKE THE BOSS'S CAR

July 10 1965,
Silverstone (Great Britain)

For the 1965 British Grand Prix at Silverstone Brabham's drivers Dan Gurney (photo - right) and Jack Brabham qualified seventh and eighth respectively. At the end of the warm-up lap, Gurney's Climax engine dropped a valve. On the grid, teammate and team owner Jack Brabham offered his own car to the American, and Brabham watched the race from the pits. Gurney finished sixth.

LOTUS BOSS RELEASED AFTER NIGHT IN JAIL

July 20 1965, Haarlem Court House (Holland)

Lotus driver Jim Clark and team principal Colin Chapman had a difficult relationship with the Dutch police in Zandvoort. While mechanics worked on his car in the pits during practice for the 1963 Dutch Grand Prix, Jim Clark was watching practice from the Tarzan corner. Despite having the correct pass, local police decided the World Championship leader was in a place reserved for photographers, and an officer grabbed him by his jacket, attempting to drag him away. The Lotus driver's overalls were torn, and Clark said about the incident: "I wasn't doing any harm and there was an 'international incident' until someone explained to the policeman that I was entitled to be where I was." Two years later the Dutch police failed to see Lotus team principal Colin Chapman's pass and tried to force him off the grid with minutes to go before the start. Chapman, who had the pass on his belt rather than around the neck, allegedly hit the officer and was manhandled by several policemen after the race. They tore his shirt apart and according to some witnesses also hit his wife Hazel in the face. Chapman spent the night in jail in Zandvoort and was taken to court in Haarlem on the Tuesday after the race. Here, the case was adjourned as it involved too many witnesses, and nothing was ever heard of it again. Despite the problems with the police, Jim Clark and Lotus won the Dutch Grand Prix in both 1963 and 1965.

41 LEAD CHANGES

September 12 1965, Monza (Italy)

The 1965 Italian Grand Prix in Monza saw the lead change 41 times in the course of 76 laps. At the time, there were no chicanes at the high-speed track outside Milan and slipstreaming was the order of the day. Jim Clark (Lotus-Climax), John Surtees (Ferrari) and BRM teammates Jackie Stewart and Graham Hill all took turns at the lead, which for a long time changed almost every lap. Stewart was in his first season in F1 and Monza was the first experience of wheel-to-wheel slipstreaming. He adapted himself splendidly and was leading twice as often as his rivals. Surtees dropped out after 34 laps with clutch problems and Jim Clark, who had clinched the World Championship six weeks earlier at the German Grand Prix, stopped in the Lesmo corner on lap 64. He got out of the car, kicked the fuel pump and drove slowly back to the pits to retire. This left BRM teammates Stewart and Hill at the front, and the two Brits fought hard in the closing laps. When Hill got slightly sideways in one of the last corners on the final lap, Stewart gained sufficient advantage to score his first Grand Prix win (photo).

THE VIEW OF A F1 DRIVER

May 19 1966, Monte Carlo (Monaco)

How is the view from the cockpit of a F1 car in Monte Carlo? An ambitious photographer decided to find out in 1966, and BRM driver Jackie Stewart agreed to help. A Nikon camera - presumably with a self-timer! - was mounted on a special helmet, and Stewart used it for a few laps during practice.

CALL OF NATURE

June 12 1966,
Spa-Francorchamps (Belgium)

In 1966 Dan Gurney, already a Grand Prix winner for Porsche and Brabham, founded AAR Eagle, his own Formula 1 team. The first Eagle was ready to fly in the Belgian Grand Prix, but the planned Weslake V12 engine was not yet available. To put some mileage on the chassis, Gurney mounted a 2.8 litre, four-cylinder Coventry Climax into the first Eagle, but the car was hopelessly underpowered at the fast Spa-Francorchamps circuit and produced a lot of vibrations. Gurney qualified the Eagle in last position, and in the race, he had to stop to relieve himself in a ditch beside the circuit. He wedged a big stone under one of the wheels and left the engine ticking over while he answered the urgent call of nature. "The vibrations got to me – I was fearful something was going to burst inside," he explained later. He was classified seventh, five laps after the winner John Surtees (Ferrari). A year later Gurney was back in Spa-Francorchamps with the Eagle, by then with the Weslake V12 engine, and he won the team's only Grand Prix victory in dominant fashion.

STEWART INTRODUCE SAFETY BELTS

June 12 1966, Spa-Francorchamps (Belgium)

In the 1966 Belgian Grand Prix in Spa-Francorchamps, BRM driver Jackie Stewart became the first driver to use safety belts in Formula 1. “I had just come back from the Indianapolis 500, where safety belts were compulsory. I didn't like them to begin with, but I had the whole month of May to get used to them, and in the end, it was clear to me that they could be really helpful. So, when I returned to Europe, I had safety belts fitted to my F1 car,” Stewart says.

HOLLYWOOD INVADES FORMULA 1

1966, Various Circuits

In 1966 Metro-Goldwyn-Mayer (MGM) produced one of Hollywood's most expensive films to date. Directed by John Frankenheimer, 'Grand Prix' was the story of four drivers fighting for the Formula 1 World Championship, of their women and of their cars. The cast included 1960s superstars James Garner, Yves Montand, Françoise Hardy and Eva Marie Saint. In the course of five months, the crew of 200 filmed in six different countries, at most of the 1966 Grands Prix. The 1961 World Champion Phil Hill drove a modified camera car in some of the practice sessions for the Monaco and Belgian Grands Prix. For additional footage, a 'ghost' Grand Prix was staged in Clermont-Ferrand in France. For this, Frankenheimer imported some 40 of the top drivers and the motoring press. The cars used were mocked-up Formula 3 cars made to look like contemporary F1 cars, and during the season, Frankenheimer and MGM owned the biggest private racing team in the world. The budget for 'Grand Prix' was $10 million, but the film won three Oscars, for Best Sound Effects, Best Film Editing and Best Sound.

WORLD CHAMPION HIT BY BIRD

July 3 1966, Reims (France)

World Champion Jim Clark did not take part in the 1966 French Grand Prix. During Thursday practice at Reims when the Scotsman was going at close to 250 km/h on the Soissons Straight a bird crashed into him and smashed his goggles. Clark was immediately flown to London for examination by an eye specialist. The World Champion was extremely lucky to escape with severe bruising and a black eye. Clark had had a fear for birds ever since his Lotus team-mate Alan Stacey was killed after a pheasant hit him in the face during the 1960 Belgian Grand Prix in Spa-Francorchamps.

A F1 CAR WITH TWO ENGINES

September 4 1966, Monza (Italy)

The British BRM team had been very successful in the 1.5-litre formula between 1961 and 1965 with Graham Hill winning the 1962 title and finishing runner-up in 1963, 1964 and 1965. When the new 3.0-litre formula was introduced in 1966, BRM decided to create a new engine by linking two of their successful 1.5-litre V8 engines on their sides, bottom end to bottom end, linked by the crankshaft. This created a 3.0-litre H16. By carrying over most of the components, the H16 was in some ways a simple solution. But it also created an enormous monster of an engine, which was both complicated and heavy. With the H16 the BRMs were more than 120 kgs heavier than the opposition. The H16 engine made its debut in the 1966 Italian Grand Prix with Graham Hill and Jackie Stewart driving the BRMs. They both retired from the race – and both BRM drivers also retired from the remaining two Grands Prix of the season. Things did not really improve in 1967, but the BRM H16 did actually win a race: Lotus was waiting for Ford's new V8 Cosworth, in 1966 and early 1967 and opted to use the BRM engine and Jim Clark won the 1966 United States Grand Prix in a Lotus-BRM, on a day when most of the frontrunners retired. The H16 was quietly forgotten after the 1967 season: it was too big, too heavy, too thirsty and too complicated.

"It would have been better used as a ship's anchor than as a F1 power plant," is how Jackie Stewart remembers the BRM H16.

HOT START

September 4 1966,
Monza (Italy)

The 1966 Italian Grand Prix at Monza got off to a hot start. Mike Parkes had qualified in pole position, but it was his Ferrari teammate Lorenzo Bandini who led the first lap. Parkes took the lead on lap two but on lap three it was John Surtees (Cooper-Maserati) who crossed the line in first place. The fourth lap saw the fourth leader with Jack Brabham (Brabham-Repco) in front. But none of the four early leaders won the race: After 68 laps it was Ferrari's Lodovico Scarfiotti (photo) who took a popular home win.

"SO – YOU THINK YOU'RE SO SMART?"

January 2 1967, Kyalami (South Africa)

Franco Lini (photo -left) was one of Italy's leading F1 journalists in the 1960s. He was never afraid of giving Enzo Ferrari and his team a hard time. The 1965-1966 period was not a successful time for the Scuderia, and at Ferrari's annual press conference, Lini and Enzo Ferrari had shouting matches. Perhaps old Enzo realised that Lini's criticism was justified, or maybe he just got tired of the stubborn journalist, but in late 1966, and very much out of the blue, Enzo Ferrari offered Lini the job of team manager. Franco accepted and from the opening round of the 1967 Formula 1 World Championship in South Africa, he was in charge. With Mauro Forghieri as technical director, Lini ran the team in the 1967 and 1968 seasons. Results did not improve, and he re-turned to journalism when his two-year contract with Ferrari expired.

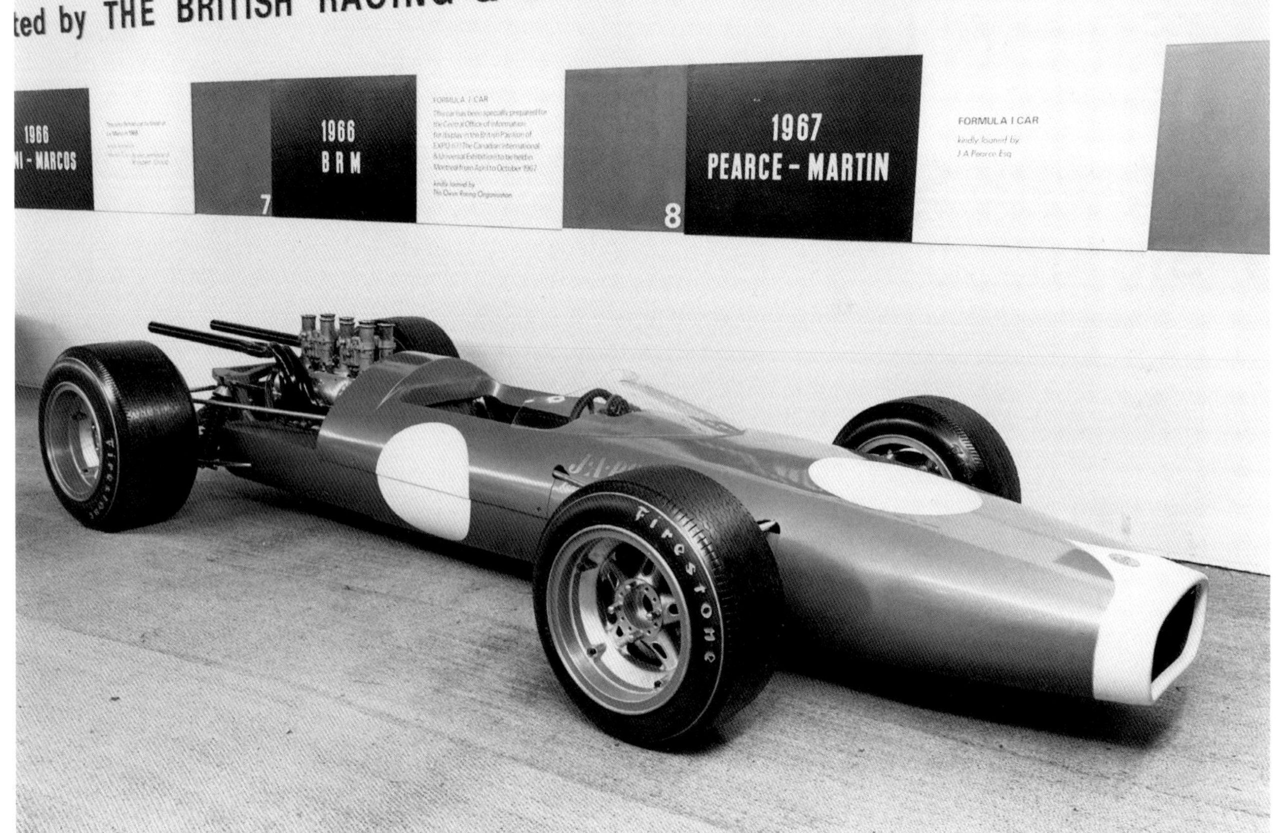

AN ENTIRE TEAM GOES UP IN FLAMES

April 25 1967,
Silverstone (Great Britain)

J. A. Pearce was a West London based wheeler-dealer with a passion for racing. He was also a skilled welder, and he produced two space frame Formula 1 chassis for 1967. Powered by the obscure Martin V8 engine, the Pearce F1 car was launched at the London Racing Car Show and the team was ready to make its debut in the non-championship International Trophy in Silverstone in late April 1967. On the Wednesday night before the race, the team's transporter – parked well away from everybody else in the Silverstone paddock – suddenly caught fire. Before the fire-fighters got there, the F1 cars and the transporter became molten metal. The fire was so intense, that considerable damage was done to the tarmac (which was used as the straight during Silverstone club meetings). When mechanics from other teams arrived in the Silverstone paddock the following morning, they were surprised to see the partially-melted F1 cars in the transporter wreckage – but no sign of any tools. The conclusion that most people came to was that the Pearce mechanics had removed their toolboxes from the transporter before the fire.
Luckily, the team was very well insured...

FERRARI STAGE DEAD HEAT IN SICILY

May 21 1967, Siracusa (Italy)

The 1967 non-championship race in Siracusa on Sicily had a poor entry list with only seven cars lining up in the grid. But the crowd was happy, as Ferrari – who had lost team leader Lorenzo Bandini only two weeks earlier in a tragic accident in Monaco – sent two cars for Lodovico Scarfiotti and Mike Parkes. The red cars dominated from start to finish and it was clear team-orders would decide the race. The spectators made loud appeals to team principal Franco Lini to let local Italian Scarfiotti win, but it was decided to have a dead heat. Scarfiotti and Parkes spent the last few laps rehearsing how to cross the line side by side, and on the final lap they got it just right. They staged a perfect dead heat with both drivers credited with exactly identical times of 1h40m58.4s.

A FORMULA 2 CAR OUT-QUALIFIES ALL BUT TWO F1 CARS

August 5 1967, Nürburgring (Germany)

The 22-year-old Jacky Ickx was the star of qualifying for the 1967 German Grand Prix at the Nürburgring. In order to get a sufficient number of cars for the 22.835 km long circuit, a handful of 1.6-litre Formula 2 cars were allowed to join the 3.0-litre Formula 1 cars and the young Belgian qualified his F2 Matra third overall – ahead of 11 F1 cars! Ickx's incredible lap was 20.9 seconds faster than the next F2 car, the Lotus of Jackie Oliver. As the F2 cars were classified separately, Ickx would only start on 'pole position' in the F2 field and he lined up behind the slowest F1 car – the Brabham-Repco of Guy Ligier. Which had qualified more than a minute slower than Ickx.

FOUR CARS ON THE FRONT ROW

August 6 1967, Nürburgring (Germany)

Since 1973 there have only been two cars on each row of the Formula 1 starting grid and since 1980 the grid has been 'staggered' with the faster car on each row starting slightly ahead of the other car. But in the 1950s and 1960s there were three or even four cars on the front row. The last race with four cars on the front row was the 1967 German Grand Prix at the Nürburgring with Jim Clark (Lotus-Ford), Denny Hulme (Brabham-Repco), Jackie Stewart (BRM) and Dan Gurney (Eagle) starting beside each other.

ARRIVING IN AN AMBULANCE

August 27 1967, Mosport Park (Canada)

In the 1960s, Formula 1 was a risky business, and it was not unusual for a driver to leave the circuit in an ambulance. But arriving in an ambulance for the start of a Grand Prix was unusual. This happened to reigning World Champion Jack Brabham at the 1967 Canadian Grand Prix at the Mosport International Raceway, in Bowmanville close to Toronto. It was Canada's first Grand Prix and the race was part of the country's centennial celebrations. Interest was high and 55,000 spectators – at the time the largest crowd ever to see a sporting event in Canada – attended the race. Bumper-to-bumper traffic on the roads leading to the circuit meant Brabham almost missed the race, but the quick-thinking Australian abandoned his car and begged an ambulance driver to help. They arrived at the track minutes before the start with lights blazing and sirens blaring. Brabham remained cool, calm and collected and after 2 hours and 40 minutes he took the chequered flag to win the race.

A ONE-RACE F1 CAREER WITH FERRARI

October 22 1967,
Mexico City (Mexico)

Jonathan Williams (photo - right) was looking forward to a nice holiday in southern California in October 1967. The previous year, the relatively unknown Englishman had been signed by Ferrari for the Scuderia's Formula 2 and sportscar programmes. The F2 car proved uncompetitive, and Williams was left with just a few sports car races. After the October 15 CanAm Series race at Laguna Seca, Williams had almost two weeks to enjoy a Ferrari Spider road car, Californian sunshine and local girlfriends before the next CanAm race at Riverside on October 29. Then he got a call from Ferrari to get down to Mexico City for the final Formula 1 Grand Prix of the season. Ferrari had only entered Chris Amon, and Williams spent the Friday watching the New Zealander from the pits. On Saturday, he was asked to have a go in Amon's spare car, and he qualified 16th. In the race, Williams's unexpected Formula 1 debut ended with eighth place.

"In those days, it meant you went round the back of the pits and shot yourself – whereas today if you finished eighth, you would think it was terrific," he said later. Eighth place was certainly not enough to impress the Ferrari management, and Jonathan Williams was quietly dropped from the Scuderia after going off in the first corner of the CanAm race in Riverside a week later.

ONLY FIVE CARS AFTER LAP 16

May 26 1968, Monte Carlo (Monaco)

Formula One is always exciting, but the spectators at the 1968 Monaco Grand Prix witnessed one of the less interesting races in the history of the sport. Only 16 cars were allowed to start on the narrow street circuit and the first laps saw several drivers crashing out or retiring with mechanical problems. By the end of the 16th lap, only five were still running! At the finish, only Graham Hill (photo) and Richard Attwood (BRM) had completed the full distance of 80 laps. Cooper-BRM teammates Lucien Bianchi and Lodovico Scarfiotti, in third and fourth place, were four laps behind the winner and the last finisher, Denny Hulme (McLaren-Ford) was a further three laps down.

ALL IN (HALF) A SEASON'S WORK

July 7 1968, Rouen (France)

Vic Elford's F1 debut was impressive. From 17th and last place on the grid, he finished the wet 1968 French Grand Prix in a solid fourth place in a Cooper-BRM. But even more impressive were his results leading up to the F1 debut: In January, Elford won the Rallye Monte Carlo in a Porsche 911. The following weekend Elford was again driving a Porsche – but this time in a 907 prototype and the race was the Daytona 24 Hours. Elford (partnered by Jochen Neerpasch, Rolf Stommelen, Jo Siffert and Hans Herrmann) won again. In early May he lost 16 minutes on the first lap of the Targa Florio due to a tyre failure on his Porsche 907, but he still won the race with co-driver Umberto Maglioli. Two weeks later, in a Porsche 908 and partnered by Siffert, he won the Nürburgring 1000 kms. And then came fourth place in his F1 debut at Rouen!

GLAD TO BE ALIVE

August 4 1968,
Nürburgring (Germany)

Dark clouds hung over the Nürburgring in more ways than one before the 1968 German Grand Prix. On the same weekend of the four previous months, an F1 driver had been killed: on April 7, Jim Clark lost his life in a F2 race at Hockenheim; on May 7 Mike Spence died after an accident in practice for the Indianapolis 500; on June 8 Lodovico Scarfiotti perished in an accident during the Rossfeld hillclimb; and on July 7 Jo Schlesser did not survive when his Honda caught fire in the French Grand Prix. Now it was August 4 and the German Grand Prix was about to start in fog and rain at the dangerous Nürburgring.

"That race should never have been held – the spray was absolutely unbelievable. I couldn't see anything at all." Jackie Stewart said later. "Even in perfect conditions, the Nürburgring really was a ridiculous place – the most dangerous circuit in the world, where over 100 people had been killed over the years."

The Scot, the most safety conscious driver at the time, went on to dominate the race, and when he crossed the line in his Matra-Ford, he was more than four minutes ahead of Graham Hill. Despite the horrendous weather and the dangerous conditions, all 20 drivers survived the race.

TWO RED-EYE FLIGHTS, NO RACE

September 8 1968, Monza (Italy)

American Mario Andretti made a sensational start to his F1 career in practice for the 1968 Italian Grand Prix. He was fastest in the opening practice in his works Lotus and when qualifying started, he immediately rushed out to do the stipulated eight laps, which would give him eighth place at the end of the day. He then pitted, ran to a waiting helicopter with fellow-American Bobby Unser (who was making his F1 debut with BRM), and flew to Milan's Malpensa airport, where a private jet took them to Geneva. There, the Americans boarded a scheduled flight to the United States, where they raced in the Hoosier 100 at Indianapolis Raceway Park on the Saturday, with Andretti finishing second behind A. J. Foyt.

Another series of flights took Andretti and Unser back to the Italian Grand Prix. Arriving in Monza on Sunday morning, ready to race, they were met by bad news from the organisers: While Andretti and Unser had been in the States, the organisers had decided to invoke a rule which prevented drivers from participating in two international races within 24 hours.

TWO TEAMS IN ONE WEEKEND

November 3 1968, Mexico City (Mexico)

Joakim Bonnier entered his own privateer McLaren-BRM for the 1968 Mexican Grand Prix. The Swedish veteran was only 17th fastest in the first practice session on Friday. During practice, the BRM engine dropped a valve, and it looked like Bonnier would be a non-starter. Honda's only driver in Mexico was John Surtees, but the Japanese team had brought a spare car, and on Saturday, they offered this to Bonnier. The Swede switched cars and improved his Friday time by 2.5 seconds and went on to finish fifth in the race. In 2022 Nyck de Vries did something similar in the Italian Grand Prix: The Dutchman made a 'Young Driver' appearance for Aston Martin in the FP1 practice, and when Alex Albon had to be operated for appendicitis, he took over the Thai's Williams on Saturday. In the race, de Vries's F1 debut, he finished ninth.

May 4 1969,
Barcelona (Spain)

A DOMINANT WIN

Jackie Stewart's win in the 1969 Spanish Grand Prix at the Montjuich street circuit in Barcelona was the most dominant in the history of the Formula 1 World Championship. The Tyrrell Matra-Ford driver was two laps in front of Bruce McLaren in second place at the chequered flag. Damon Hill (Williams-Renault) was also two laps ahead of second-placed Olivier Panis (Ligier-Mugen/Honda in the 1995 Australian Grand Prix, but the Adelaide street circuit was shorter than the Montjuic circuit.

DOWN TO THE LETTER

May 9 1969, Geneva (Switzerland)

Jochen Rindt was busy at the typewriter in early May. The Lotus driver was lucky to survive a spectacular crash in the Spanish Grand Prix in Montjuic Park on May 4, and a few days later he wrote letters to both his team boss Colin Chapman and the English weekly Autosport. The crash was caused by the rear wing collapsing, and in his letter to Autosport, Rindt wrote: "Wings have nothing to do with a motor car" and "wings are very dangerous and should be banned." The letter to Chapman was even more serious. Rindt noted that he had now been in F1 for five years and usually managed to stay out of trouble. But "this situation changed rapidly since I joined your team." Rindt suggested that the Lotus cars were too fragile, writing "your cars are so quick that we would still be competitive with a few extra pounds to make the weakest parts stronger." He finished his letter with the words: "I can only drive a car in which I have some confidence, and I feel the point of no confidence is quite near." Tragically, Rindt was killed 16 months later in an accident most likely initiated by a failure in his Lotus right front brake during practice for the 1970 Italian Grand Prix in Monza. Before the accident, he had scored enough points to be crowned World Champion posthumously.

WINGS BANNED DURING PRACTICE

May 16 1969, Monte Carlo (Monaco)

The FIA's sporting commission (CSI) made significant changes to the Formula 1 regulations during practice for the 1969 Monaco Grand Prix. When practice started on Thursday, most of the cars featured the high wings, which had first been introduced during the 1968 season. Dramatic accidents in the Spanish GP, the race before Monaco, caused by these collapses worried both the CSI and the organisers in Monaco. The CSI met on Thursday night to discuss the matter and after long talks it was decided to ban the high wings with immediate effect. Small fins ahead of the front wheels and small wings behind the driver were still allowed. Most team owners were happy to see the dangerous wings go, but Tyrrell-Matra team principal Ken Tyrrell protested strongly, arguing that his cars were designed around the high wings. Still, when Friday practice started at 07.50, all the wings had been removed from the cars, and Jackie Stewart dominated both practice and Saturday's qualifying in one of Tyrrell's Matras. Friday's wing-less times were less than a second a lap slower than the Thursday times with wings.

PRIVATEER LOTUS ON LOAN TO WORKS TEAM

July 17 1969,
Silverstone (Great Britain)

On paper, Team Lotus looked strong in 1969. Graham Hill was the reigning World Champion and Jochen Rindt was one of Formula 1's up-and-coming stars. The Lotus 49B was still competitive. And – the new 4WD Lotus 63 was waiting in the wings.

In early summer, Lotus boss Colin Chapman was convinced that the new 4WD car would become a world beater. He sold most of the team's conventional 49Bs – one of them had won the Monaco Grand Prix a few weeks earlier with Hill behind the wheel – to privateers like Sweden's Joakim Bonnier. But Rindt refused to drive the unreliable Lotus 63 in the British Grand Prix. He drove the team's one remaining 49B. After the first practice day, Hill quietly suggested that the old 49B would be more competitive, and this left Chapman with a problem. In the end, Bonnier was persuaded to lend his newly-acquired 49B to Hill and the Swede could instead earn his starting money in the Englishman's troublesome 63 (photo).

DISQUALIFIED FOR BEING TOO SLOW

September 20 1969, Mosport (Canada)

'Insufficient speed' was the reason given when Al Pease was black-flagged from the 1969 Canadian Grand Prix. The local hero - in a four-year-old Eagle - had started the race from the back of the grid after setting a time some 11.1 seconds slower than Jacky Ickx (Brabham) on pole position. On the first lap, the Canadian was involved in an incident which saw the Brabham of Silvio Moser crash heavily. Pease was lapped for the first time after only four laps and there were several close calls when the fast boys had to pass him again and again. After 22 of the 90 laps Race Control had had enough, and Pease was disqualified for being too slow. It was the end of the Canadian's short Formula 1 career, which included three World Championship Grands Prix - all in Canada and all in the Eagle from 1966. He finished in 1967 but was not classified as he was 43 laps behind the winner after a difficult race with several technical problems. In 1968 engine problems in practice meant he did not start the race and then came the embarrassing 1969 race.

70's

FROM PRISON TO THE GRID AND BACK

June 7 1970, Spa-Francorchamps (Belgium)

Ronnie Peterson, who had made his Formula 1 debut only a few weeks earlier in Monaco, almost missed the start of the 1970 Belgian Grand Prix. The race was delayed for a few minutes so the Swede could make it to the grid - and he came straight from a prison cell! Peterson had overslept in the morning and was late away from his hotel. On his way to the circuit, Peterson's Mercedes landed up in a line of cars, which only crept forward at very slow speed. He put his foot down and drove fast to the end of the queue, where a policeman waved at him. Peterson thought the policeman wanted him to go ahead, but this was clearly a misunderstanding - the policeman tried to stop him. When the policeman looked away, the Swede made one of his famous racing starts and headed for the circuit. "The policeman accused me of having driven over his foot, but that was a lie," Peterson said later. A motorcycle cop chased him and when Peterson was finally pulled over, he was taken to the local police station and locked up. BRM team principal Louis Stanley, who was famous for having all the right connections, was asked for help. He immediately contacted the Belgian Minister of Interior, who was attending the race. The politician made a few phone calls and Peterson was released. "The organisers were understanding," Stanley said. "The start was delayed for a few minutes and the jailbird arrived on the track with motorcycle police escorts and flashing lights to be reunited with his car." Peterson retired from the race after 20 laps, and when he returned to the pits, the police were waiting for him. Still in his overalls, the March driver was taken to a prison in Liege, where he spent the night. The case was then quietly forgotten.

HOCKENHEIM ORGANISES A GRAND PRIX IN JUST THREE WEEKS

August 2 1970, Hockenheim (Germany)

The 1970 German Grand Prix at the Nürburgring was scheduled for August 2, but the Grand Prix Drivers Association (GPDA) asked for several modifications to be carried out on the 22.8 km long Nordschleife – such as a marshal with a fire extinguisher at every corner. The organisers replied that this was impossible as there were 135 corners on the circuit. Three weeks before the race, the GPDA informed the race organisers that its members were not prepared to race at the Nürburgring. The race was cancelled on July 8. A couple of days later, the Automobilclub von Deutschland (AvD) announced that the 1970 'Grosser Preis von Deutschland' would now take place at the Hockenheim circuit – on its original date, August 2, just three weeks later. The race was won by Jochen Rindt (Lotus). On the same day the AvD also held the (Not So Grosser) 'Preis von Deutschland' for Formula 2 cars at the Nürburgring.

F1 CARS AND TRANSPORTER IMPOUNDED BY POLICE

August 17 1970,
German/Austrian border

When the March team returned from the 1970 Austrian Grand Prix at the Österreichring, their transporter was shadowed discreetly by a police helicopter. As soon as the transporter, carrying the cars of Chris Amon and Jo Siffert, crossed the border into Germany, it was stopped by the local police and confiscated.

The story began two weeks earlier when Hubert Hahne had failed to qualify a private March for the German Grand Prix at Hockenheim. Hahne - second in the European Formula 2 Championship 1969 - had bought a brand-new March with support from the powerful Alex Springer Verlag and Bild Zeitung, but he was never even close to qualifying for his home race. He was convinced he had been swindled and that he had been sold an inferior car. His solicitor issued writs against March and the German police impounded the March transporter as soon as it arrived on German soil. on its way back to the team HQ in Bicester in England. It took March team principal Max Mosley three days to get the transporter released by the German authorities. He had to promise Hahne that his car would be tested thoroughly by one of the work drives. In September 1970 Hahne took his March to Silverstone. He wanted proof that the car was competitive, and Mosley had agreed that works driver Ronnie Peterson (photo) would drive it. If the Swede could manage lap times similar to those he had done in his own March, Hahne would rest his case. In Hahne's car Peterson, a Formula 1 novice with just seven Grands Prix under his belt, quickly got down to the lap times set with his own car. And then went almost two seconds faster. Hahne returned to Germany and announced his retirement a few days later.

A MAN IN A HURRY

August 22 1970, Oulton Park (Great Britain

Jochen Rindt was a man in a hurry in 1970. After four Grand Prix wins in a row during the summer, the Lotus driver was leading the World Championship by a large margin. Between the Austrian and the Italian Grand Prix, he took part in the non-championship Gold Cup race at Oulton Park on Saturday August 22. The Austrian seemed keen to spend the Sunday with his family, and as soon as he had taken the chequered flag in second place, he stopped his car at the Old Hall corner. He crossed the track to pick up his suitcase, which he had left with marshals before the race. Rindt was in his plane on the circuit's airstrip and on his way to Vienna as race winner John Surtees finished his slowing down lap. A few days later Rindt was killed in practice for the Italian Grand Prix, but his point tally was not beaten, and he was posthumously awarded the 1970 World Championship.

THE AMAZING STORY OF CHASSIS 5

September 6 1970, Monza (Italy)

The Lotus 72 was ahead of its times when it made its debut in 1970, and it went on to win 20 Grands Prix and the Drivers' World Championship in 1970 (with Jochen Rindt) and 1972 (with Emerson Fittipaldi) as well as the Constructors' title in 1970, 1972 and 1973. The story of chassis number 5 is especially remarkable. It made its debut in the 1970 Italian Grand Prix with newcomer Fittipaldi behind the wheel. When team leader Jochen Rindt was killed during practice, Lotus withdrew its cars from the race, but the team returned for the United States Grand Prix, where Fittipaldi won with the car. Fittipaldi also raced Lotus 72-5 in 1971 and used it to clinch the 1972 World Championship at the Italian Grand Prix. The Brazilian raced 72-5 in 1973 as well, and when he left the team in 1974, his successor Jacky Ickx used it for most of the season. The Belgian continued with it – now five years old – in the early part of 1975. When Ickx left the team at midseason,72-5 was taken over by Brian Henton. The Englishman was behind the wheel when the car made its final appearance at the 1975 United States Grand Prix – more than five years and exactly 1,856 days after its debut in the 1970 Italian Grand Prix.

CHAOS IN MEXICO

October 25 1970, Mexico City (Mexico)

A much bigger crowd than in the past – estimated at over 200,000 – turned the 1970 Mexican Grand Prix into chaos. Keen to see the action, the crowd began to break down fences during the support races on Sunday morning. Spectators were sitting on the Armco barriers, and reigning World Champion Jackie Stewart and local hero Pedro Rodriguez went round the circuit in a road car and pleaded with the fans to move back. "We were using a loud hailer, Pedro speaking in Spanish, me in English," Stewart said later. "We were trying to explain that they were endangering not only their own lives but ours as well, and surprisingly, they began to move back. Only they couldn't get over the barriers. The people behind the fences refused to move and give up their view, and so there was pushing and shoving going on."

For a long time, it seemed that there would not be a race, but the organisers feared that cancellation would cause a riot, and eventually the race was started an hour and 15 minutes late. During the race, spectators again crept up to the edge of the road, and many of them crossed the track during the race. Jackie Stewart retired ("I hit a bloody great dog on one of the fastest parts of the track"), and towards the end of the race, the scene was described as "a circuit lined with human guard-rails." It was a miracle no spectators were hurt.
It was the last Mexican Grand Prix for 16 years.

HELMET CHANGE

March 6 1971,
Kyalami (South Africa)

When Howden Ganley's BRM developed a misfire in the 1971 South African Grand Prix, the New Zealander was somewhat relieved. He dived into the pits, and while the mechanics tried to keep the mechanical fuel pump alive by pouring water on it, Ganley jumped out of the car and grabbed his old open-face helmet. He had started the race wearing a new full-face helmet, but this was much heavier than his old open-face helmet. The added weight and the shortage of oxygen in the high-altitude of Kyalami had made him weary. With the old open-face helmet he was soon up to speed again, but sadly the BRM gave up shortly after half-distance.

THREE DIFFERENT CARS

April 9 1971,
Oulton Park (Great Britain)

In the 1960s and early 1970s, it was not unusual for a team to enter three cars for a race. Lotus did that for the 1971 non-championship race at Oulton Park in England. What was unusual was the fact that the three cars for Emerson Fittipaldi, Reine Wisell and Tony Trimmer were all very different. Fittipaldi (photo) was in the contemporary Lotus 72 while Wisell was in the team's experimental 56B – complete with 4WD and a gas-turbine engine. Trimmer was in a Lotus 49C, originally introduced in 1970. When Trimmer crashed the car during practice, the team found spare bits from another 49C – which was on display in Normands Garage some 100 kms from Oulton Park!

RAIN STOPS RUNNER-UP

May 22 1971, Monte Carlo (Monaco)

Mario Andretti enjoyed a great start to the 1971 season. He won his very first race for Ferrari, the season-opener in Kyalami, South Africa. Mario then retired during the second round in Spain but was still second in the World Championship behind Jackie Stewart when he arrived in Monaco for round three. In the Friday session, which also counted for the grid, the distributor drove on his Ferrari sheared, and he was unable to set a competitive time. When it rained in Saturday's final session, he was unable to qualify.

FULL DISTANCE = 12 LAPS

August 1 1971, Nürburgring (Germany)

The Nürburgring Nordschleife was one of the most spectacular circuits in the history of the Formula 1 World Championship - which was just as well, because the spectators did not get many chances to see each car. With a lap of 22.835 km, the 1971 German Grand Prix at the Nordschleife lasted only 12 laps (274.020 km). This is the Grand Prix planned for the fewest number of laps. The 2021 Belgian Grand Prix at Spa-Francorchamps was planned for 44 laps, but was stopped due to heavy rain, and officially only lasted one lap. The record for most laps was held by the United States Grands Prix 1963-1965, which all consisted of 110 laps @ 3.700 km of Watkins Glen.

FRONT TO BACK

September 4 1971,
Monza (Italy):

Aerodynamics was still in its infancy in 1971, but it was clear that wings increased grip in the corners. It was also clear that the wings increased drag (which reduced top speed) on the straights. In practice for the 1971 Italian Grand Prix in Monza – in those days without chicanes and all about high-speed – many different solutions were tested. Cars ran without front wings, without rear wings, with no wings at all. And then there was McLaren: It was decided that the conventional front and rear wings increased drag too much – but a little extra grip would be welcome in the corners. The solution: the small front wings were removed – and used during practice as mini rear wings on Jackie Oliver's car.

HANDS UP - CLOSE FINISH AHEAD

September 5 1971, Monza (Italy)

The 1971 Italian Grand Prix saw the closest finish in the history of the Formula 1 World Championship. As the last lap began, five drivers were still in with a chance to win the race, and everything was decided in the Parabolica, the final corner.

François Cevert (Tyrrell) was leading going into the corner with Ronnie Peterson (March) almost alongside him. Both braked late - very late. This gave Peter Gethin (BRM) the chance he was looking for, and the Englishman went for the inside and in the sprint to the chequered flag, he just held on to the lead. He finished 0.01 second in front of Peterson and 0.09 second in front of Cevert in third place. Mike Hailwood (Surtees) was fourth, 0.18 second behind Gethin and Howden Ganley (BRM) fifth, a full 0.61 second behind. "I knew it was going to be really close", Gethin said. "They are excitable chaps, the Italians, and I reckon they might not be too clever with their timekeeping. There were no TV replays in those days, so I thought that if I raised my arm just before the line, they would give me the win no matter what."

THE FIRST RED FLAG

September 19 1971, Mosport Park (Canada)

The 1971 Canadian Grand Prix at Mosport Park (photo) started late in the afternoon because of a tragic accident in the Formula Ford support race. Five drivers and a group of marshals were involved in an accident on the first lap. When the rest of the field arrived at the accident scene on lap two, local driver Wayne Kelly lost control of his Titan and crashed into an ambulance which was stopped at the side of the track. Kelly's car slid under the ambulance, and he was killed instantly. When the Formula 1 race was eventually started, it was raining, and soon thick fog arrived. It got worse, and when marshals could not see their colleagues in the next corner, it was decided to stop the race after 64 of the scheduled 80 laps.

It was the first time in Formula 1 history a Grand Prix was red-flagged.

WHEN VW WAS IN F1

October 3 1971, Watkins Glen (United States)

The Volkswagen group has contemplated Formula 1 several times, but only in 2026 will Audi officially enter the sport. But from 1969 to 1971 a team officially named 'Pete Lovely Volkswagen' entered a total of nine Grands Prix. American Pete Lovely made his debut in the Formula 1 World Championship back in 1960, when he finished 11th in a private Cooper-Ferrari in the United States Grand Prix. Nine years later he was back, this time in a private Lotus 49, which he raced in the Canadian, US and Mexican Grands Prix; finishing seventh in Canada. The car was entered by 'Pete Lovely Volkswagen', but the German manufacturer was not really involved: Lovely opened a VW dealership in Fife, Washington in 1954 and ran it for 34 years. When he needed an entrant for his private Lotus in a handful of 1969-1971 Grands Prix, his own company was the obvious choice.

HURRICANE GINGER AND THE PRANCING HORSE

October 3 1971, Watkins Glen (United Stated)

On the morning of the 1971 United States Grand Prix, Mario Andretti (photo - left) prayed for bad weather. Not so much at Watkins Glen, where he had qualified his Ferrari on the third row – but rather in Trenton, 400 km south-east of the US Grand Prix venue. Why? The American had a hectic 1971 schedule with the USAC series his main priority but also taking in as many Grands Prix as possible for Ferrari. Heavy rain on September 26 meant that the Trenton 300 USAC race was re-scheduled for October 3 - and clashed with the US Grand Prix. There was still hope for Andretti: Hurricane Ginger was moving towards Trenton, and it looked like the USAC race would have to be postponed once again. Andretti stayed in Watkins Glen, and was fourth in Friday's first qualifying session and sixth on Saturday. But when Hurricane Ginger came to nothing, he had to leave Watkins Glen and go to Trenton.
His Ferrari became a stock of spares for his teammates Jacky Ickx and Clay Regazzoni (photo - right). Andretti finished second in Trenton while Regazzoni was sixth in Watkins Glen and Ickx retired.

F1 CARAVAN

March 4 1972,
Kyalami (South Africa)

Günther Hennerici, owner of the successful Eifelland caravan empire, was a keen motor racing fan. The caravan business made him a rich man, and in 1971 he decided to set up a F1 team – the first German outfit since Porsche's withdrawal in 1963. With little time to build a chassis, Hennerici bought a March 721 and asked his friend, industrial designer Luigi Colani, to create a bodywork for what would be known as the Eifelland 21 F1 car. Colani's futuristic designs had made him famous, but he did not know much about Formula 1. When it first appeared, the Eifelland was certainly futuristic - but it was not very fast. The car made its debut in the 1972 South African Grand Prix with Rolf Stommelen behind the wheel. During practice, more and more of Colani's spectacular bodywork was replaced by more conventional March parts. This continued during the season, and the Eifelland was never a success. Hennerici lost interest, and after the Austrian Grand Prix, the entire team – the car, two engines, spares and a transporter – was sold to a certain Bernard Ecclestone, who planned to use the engines for his Brabham team and sell the rest. The price? According to Bernie "between £25,000 and £30,000."

NOT ON A SUNDAY!

May 1 1972, Jarama (Spain)

Formula 1 Grands Prix were not always held on Sundays. In fact, the very first round of the FIA Formula 1 World Championship, the 1950 British Grand Prix at Silverstone, was held on Saturday May 13. Until the mid-1980s, most British Grands Prix were held on Saturdays as was the South African Grands Prix. In 2024 the Bahrain, Saudi Arabian and Las Vegas Grand Prix are all held on Saturdays. But there were also Grands Prix which were not held during a weekend. The 1965 South African Grand Prix took place on New Year's Day, a Friday. Six Grands Prix have been held on Mondays, three in Holland (1958, 1960 and 1961) and two in South Africa (1967 and 1968). The last Grand Prix on a Monday was the 1972 Spanish Grand Prix on the Jarama circuit. This was held on May 1 - Labour Day in Europe - and a national holiday in Spain.

ONE TEAM, SIX DRIVERS

June 4 1972, Nivelles (Belgium)

With sponsorship from Marlboro, the BRM team had ambitious plans for the 1972 season – it entered no fewer than five cars for Howden Ganley, Reine Wisell, Peter Gethin, Alex Soler-Roig and Helmut Marko for the season-opener in Argentina. For the Spanish Grand Prix in May, Jean-Pierre Beltoise replaced Marko in another five-car entry. Then, in early June, BRM entered six cars for the Belgian Grand Prix in Nivelles, although Wisell had to withdraw after he broke a finger in a non-championship race the previous weekend. There were several other 1972 races with five BRMs on the entry list – a record in modern F1 history.

SHORTEST CAR CAREER EVER?

July 15 1972, Brands Hatch (Great Britain)

In 1972 Frank Williams convinced Italian toy manufacturer Politoys to sponsor his Formula 1 team. Politoys put up £40,000 for the construction of a car, and the Ford Cosworth-powered Politoys-Williams was ready for the British Grand Prix. With Frenchman Henri Pescarolo behind the wheel, the car qualified for the last place on the grid, and in the race, it was all over after just seven laps. Going through Brands Hatch's fast Dingle Dell corner, something failed – either the steering or the suspension – and the brand-new car was destroyed. The Politoys was not seen in the Formula 1 World Championship again.

FERRARI WINS, THEN WITHDRAWS FROM RACING

July 30 1972,
Modena (Italy)

When Jacky Ickx took the chequered flag ahead of team-mate Clay Regazzoni in the 1972 German Grand Prix, it was Ferrari's best F1 result for almost two years. But a few hours after the race, Enzo Ferrari announced that his team would withdraw from F1 (and sports car racing) at the end of the year. “Given the uncertainty of the coming and future times, which do not allow for a too financially burdensome programme, Ferrari is leaving its drivers free at the end of the season,” the statement said. It was not the first time the Old Man had threatened to leave the sport, and this time it only took him a few days to change his mind: the following week it was announced that Ickx had signed a new Ferrari contract to drive both in F1 and sports car racing.

A LITTLE WARM-UP

August 5 1973, Nürburgring (Germany)

As usual, the German Grand Prix in 1973 took place at the 22.835 km Nürburgring Nordschleife. What was unusual was the Sunday morning warm-up session. Not all the marshals were early risers, and there were not enough of them to man the entire circuit. Therefore, the drivers were restricted to laps on the little 2.3 km pit loop. A full complement of marshals was on hand later in the day, and the race went ahead on the Nordschleife as planned.

AND THE WINNER IS?

September 23 1973, Mosport Park (Canada)

At the 1973 Canadian Grand Prix, all three drivers on the podium believed they had won the race. It was a confusing event in both wet and dry conditions, and when Jody Scheckter (McLaren-Ford) and François Cevert (Tyrrell-Ford) crashed heavily on lap 32, a Safety Car was brought into action for the first time in the history of the Formula 1 World Championship. The problem was that it went out in front of the wrong car, and when most of the cars used the opportunity to change from rain tyres to slicks, absolute chaos was the result. At the end, Lotus boss Colin Chapman celebrated in his usual way by throwing his cap high into the air when Emerson Fittipaldi crossed the line. The Lotus-Ford driver was ushered into the victory area – but so was Peter Revson (McLaren-Ford) a few seconds later. The Shadow-Ford team also believed Jackie Oliver had won, and it took several hours and careful checking of lap charts, before an official result was announced.

This had Peter Revson as the winner, ahead of Fittipaldi and Oliver. But nobody was really sure if this was right...

MOONED AT WATKING GLEN

October 7 1973,
Watkins Glen (United States)

'Mooning' – the act of displaying one's bare buttocks – was popular in North America in the early 1970s. Still, judging from the look on Jackie Oliver's face, the Shadow driver didn't expect to be mooned on the parade lap before the 1973 United States Grand Prix. Why the spectator chose Oliver as his victim – or how he even made it onto the track – has never been explained. But the number plate of the car Oliver rode in – 'BUM 697' probably made him the obvious victim.

FOUR TEAMS IN THREE MONTHS

October 29 1973, Hethel (Great Britain):

On Monday October 29 1973 Jacky Ickx signed a contract with Lotus for 1974. The British team - winners of the 1973 Constructors' World Championship - became the Belgian's fourth team in three months.

Ickx, who had finished fourth in the 1972 World Championship for Ferrari, started the 1973 season with the Prancing Horse. But Ferrari had a bad year, and after the British Grand Prix, Ickx informed the team that he would not drive the car again until it was competitive. For the German Grand Prix on August 5, McLaren entered a third car for Ickx and he finished in a strong third place. “It was good for Mr Ferrari, too,” Ickx insisted after his first and only race for McLaren. “He will not have to ask himself anymore: ‘Is it the driver or is it the car?” The Ferrari was improved during the summer, and for the Italian Grand Prix on September 9 Ickx was back with the team, but after a disappointing eighth place, he left Maranello for good. For the last race of the 1973 season, the United States Grand Prix on October 7, Williams had entered F1 newcomer Tom Belsø. At the last minute, the Dane's place was taken by Ickx, and despite missing the first practice day because of visa problems, the Belgian took one of Williams's best 1973 results with seventh place in the race. Three weeks later Ickx signed with Lotus for 1974.

HOW TO GET INTO FORMULA 1 - BY MR E

March 2 1974,
Brasilia (Brazil)

Formula 1 was wildly popular in Brazil in the 1970s and in 1974 the country had two races. The Brazilian Grand Prix took place at Interlagos in Sao Paulo on January 27 and was won by local hero Emerson Fittipaldi in a McLaren. Many of the teams stayed in Brazil and took part in the non-championship Grande Premio Presidente Emilio Medici at the new autodromo in the capital Brasilia. This was named after the country's president, who was nearing the end of his term. The race saw Fittipaldi take another home win but it also kicked off the career of the next Brazilian World Champion. A young go kart driver by the name of Nelson Piquet Souto Maior was mad about Formula 1, and he promised the Brabham team he would help clean the cars if they could get him into the paddock. But there was a problem: they did not have a pass for him. "I said: 'Let's stick him into the boot of the car'," said Brabham owner Bernie Ecclestone. "That was Nelson's way of getting into Formula 1." Nelson Piquet went on to win the 1981 and 1983 World Championships for Brabham and a third title with Williams in 1987.

SHORTEST F1 DEBUT EVER

March 30 1974,
Kyalami (South Africa

Tom Belsø was destined to become Denmark's first Formula 1 driver in the 1974 South African Grand Prix. He qualified his Iso-Ford from the Williams team in 27th. and last position and then produced the shortest F1 debut ever: Clutch failure meant the poor Dane retired even before he had crossed the start line.

WHEN SUZUKI WAS IN F1

April 8 1974, Jarama (Spain)

Peter Agg was a successful British businessman. He was the UK importer of Lambretta scooters in the 1950s and later struck a deal with Heinkel to build and sell its three-wheeler "Bubble Car". He also became the British importer of Suzuki motorcycles, and in the early 1970s he established Trojan Racing Cars, to build CanAm customer cars for McLaren. Plans to build McLaren Formula 5000 cars under the Trojan name fell through, but Agg went ahead and built his own Formula 5000 cars, designed by ex-Brabham designer Ron Tauranac. Trojan won several F5000 races in 1973 and for 1974 Trojan also entered F1 with a Tauranac-designed car and Tim Schenken behind the wheel. The new team made its debut in the 1974 Spanish Grand Prix and carried big Suzuki stickers. But it was powered by a Ford Cosworth and the only link to the Japanese was Agg's own import business. The Suzuki sponsored Trojan entered eight races during the summer of 1974 and Schenken qualified for six of them; finishing 10th in Belgium and Austria. The team ran out of money at the end of the European season and closed down after the Italian Grand Prix.

WITH A LITTLE HELP FROM MY FRIENDS

May 16 1974, Anderstorp (Sweden)

After the 1974 Belgian Grand Prix, the Williams, Hesketh and BRM teams travelled to Anderstorp to test in preparation for the Swedish Grand Prix a month later. When Williams's Arturo Merzario did not arrive – his sportscar team Alfa Romeo needed him for testing at the Nürburgring – it seemed like a wasted journey for the team. But then James Hunt (photo) crashed his Hesketh on the first day of testing, and the car was beyond repair, and that saved Williams's day: Hunt drove the Iso-Williams for more than 50 laps and the Hesketh driver commented that it was a "lovely little motorcar – like a Rolls Royce with a very nice steering". The following week, Hunt was back in his Hesketh and Merzario in the Williams for the Monaco Grand Prix.

THE FIRST ILLEGAL START

June 9 1974,
Anderstorp (Sweden)

The 30 minutes Sunday morning warm-up before the 1974 Swedish Grand Prix was a dramatic affair. Denmark's Tom Belsø crashed his Iso Williams-Ford after a suspension failure, and it was not possible to repair the car before the race. Williams sponsor Marlboro was keen to have a Dane in the race, and less than half an hour before the start, they came to an arrangement with the other Williams driver, Richard Robarts, who gave up his car for Belsø. This was good news for another Nordic driver: Leo Kinnunen had not been able to qualify his private Surtees-Ford for the race, but with Robarts out, he moved onto the grid, and thus became the first Finn to start a World Championship Grand Prix. The second reserve, Vern Schuppan (Ensign) was also asked to tag along on the parade lap before the start, just in case another car broke down.

When Schuppan arrived on the grid, nobody told him to pull off, and he took the start with the rest of the field. He went on to finish 12th (and last) and it was only after the chequered flag, that the officials realised that there had been one car too many in the race. Schuppan was excluded from the result, although the race in Anderstorp made him the first driver to have started (and finished) a Grand Prix illegally.

NO SMOKE, NO FIRE

July 18 1974, London (Great Britain)

A mysterious, anonymous letter arrived in the offices of British weekly Autosport in the week leading up to the 1974 British Grand Prix at Brands Hatch. The letter, which was posted in Croydon in South London without a stamp, was a short message regarding the Tyrrell team and its driver Jody Scheckter: "Revenge by fire: Jody Scheckter must withdraw from Brands Hatch – if not Tyrrell-Ford F1 cars will get the same treatment as Pearce-Martin F1 cars," it said, in a clear reference to an incident in the paddock at Silverstone seven years earlier, when the new Pearce Martin team's transporter and their F1 cars inside went up in flames. The letter was handed over to the police and nothing happened to the Tyrrells during the British Grand Prix weekend – in fact Jody Scheckter won the race.

PLEASE DON'T CRASH HERE

April 27 1975,
Barcelona (Spain)

When the teams arrived for the 1975 Spanish Grand Prix in Barcelona, the safety levels at the Montjuich street circuit were completely unacceptable. Most of the armco barriers were not even bolted together properly, so the drivers went on strike. But the Spanish organisers were in a strong position. With the paddock located in a big football stadium, with only one gate which could be locked easily, they threatened to impound the teams' trucks, cars and equipment. Mechanics and even team principals spent Saturday morning tightening some of the loose bolts around the track, and qualifying went ahead. Reigning World Champion Emerson Fittipaldi (McLaren-Ford) (photo) was still not happy, and went around so slowly that he made sure he did not qualify for the race. The following day, Fittipaldi's brother Wilson (Copersucar-Ford) and Arturo Merzario (Williams-Ford) started the race but retired after the first lap in protest. Then came tragedy: on lap 26 the rear wing on Rolf Stommelen's race-leading Hill-Ford collapsed, and the German lost control. The car slid along the top of the armco and ended up on the spectators' side. Five people – three marshals, a photographer and a fireman - were killed. Stommelen was gravely injured but survived.
It was ironic that Stommelen crashed into the very section of the barriers secured by the Hill's team mechanics the day before. Jokingly, one of them had written on the Armco: "Rolf – don't crash here."

OH DEER

July 30 1975,
Nürburgring (Germany)

Hill-Ford driver Alan Jones was keen to learn the almost 23 kilometres and countless corners of the Nürburgring Nordschleife before his debut at the famous circuit in the 1975 German Grand Prix. He hired a BMW road car and started his learning process, doing lap after lap. For a long time, all went well, but then he lost control of the BMW and hit the armco – hard.

The car was badly damaged, and he later said that his first thought was: "Bloody hell – it's a hired car – what do I do here?" He pushed the BMW into a gap in the armco, and quietly disappeared. When dusk fell, he went back to the scene with colleagues James Hunt and Mark Donohue. They managed to get the car out of the Nordschleife and back onto the public roads. "The thing was crabbing like you wouldn't believe it," Jones said later. About 20 kilometres from the track, he phoned the hire car company, and told them he had crashed as he swerved to miss a deer. They came with a new car, and the quick-thinking Aussie was on his way again. On Sunday he scored his first World Championship points with a fine fifth place. Somehow, those laps in the hire car paid off...

WINNING AND CRASHING

August 17 1975, Österreichring (Austria)

Vittorio Brambilla was one of the most colourful drivers of the mid-1970s and his nickname 'The Gorilla from Monza' not only referred to his looks and hometown – it also had something to do with his aggressive driving style, which saw him crash far more often than his competitors. He started eighth in the wet 1975 Austrian Grand Prix, and most people expected him to crash sooner rather than later. But for once, the 'Gorilla' kept his orange March on the track, and drove a beautiful race, setting the fastest lap in the process. Coming up to the chequered flag and his first and only Grand Prix win, he took a hand off the steering wheel to wave to the crowd. He lost control, passed the finish line sideways and hit the armco a few metres later.

SIX APPEAL

September 22 1975, Heathrow (Great Britain

It was an unusually early launch of Tyrrell's 1976 car when the F1 media was invited to the Heathrow Hotel near London on September 22 1975. But if the date was unusual, the car was downright sensational. It was slowly unveiled from the back: conventional rear, the almost universally used Ford Cosworth engine, the usual cockpit – by then the journalists seemed almost bored. But then came two very small front wheels – and the mechanic who pulled the wraps off the car hesitates briefly. When they continued, they revealed another pair of front wheels – the Tyrrell P34 was a six-wheeler! "It is not often you have loud applause at the launch of a new F1 car. But we had with the P34," Team boss Ken Tyrrell, who was keeping secrets better than anybody else in F1, said later. The idea behind the six-wheeler was actually quite simple: with four small front wheels instead of two big ones, drag was reduced significantly. And it worked: the P34 scored a Tyrrell 1-2 win in the Swedish Grand Prix in June 1976 with Jody Scheckter and Patrick Depailler and the South African took third in the 1976 World Championship. The P34 raced on in 1977, but by then Michelin had joined Goodyear in F1, and the tyre war meant that the Americans did not have the resources to produce the special small tyres for the six-wheeler. It was the end of probably the most unusual car in F1 history, and shortly afterwards the regulations were changed: from then on, a F1 car must have four wheels.

FOR YOUR EYES ONLY - NOT!

October 5 1975, United States (United States)

Jacques Laffite (Williams) did not start the 1975 United States Grand Prix in Watkins Glen. Preparing for the race, he picked up a little bottle of what he thought was his eye drops and squirted it in both eyes. It turned out to be his visor cleaning fluid, and the Frenchman was taken to hospital in great pain.

WHEN SMOKING WAS SAFE AND SEX WAS DANGEROUS

March 14 1976,
Brands Hatch (Great Britain)

The non-championship 'Race of Champions' at Brands Hatch in March 1976 had a healthy entry with 16 cars from all the leading F1 teams. The BBC had planned extensive coverage of the race, but a few hours before the start, the cameras at the circuit were packed away. The reason: Durex, Britain's most widely used condom, had become the title sponsor for the Surtees team a few weeks before the race. The BBC was not prepared to screen pictures of a Formula 1 car with Durex stickers on it into the homes of innocent Englishmen, and the planned coverage was cancelled. "We believe family planning is a moral subject, we believe family planning is something that is here to stay and I cannot understand why the BBC has any apprehension about showing a car on TV with our brand name on it,' Durex's marketing director Bob Hall said.

Alan Jones led the first half of the race in the Durex-Surtees and finished in a strong second place to James Hunt. The Englishman was driving a Marlboro-McLaren and in third place came Jacky Ickx in a Marlboro sponsored Williams. Other teams in the race included John Player, Team Lotus and Martini Brabham. Durex produced a brilliant advert at the time, with a picture of the F1 car and the caption "The small family car".

F1 DRIVER OFFERED A GIG AT STRIP CLUB

March 28 1976, Long Beach (United States)

Jody Scheckter's 1975 United States West Grand Prix in Long Beach came to a sudden and painful end on lap 34. A fuel leak in his Tyrrell-Ford meant he had been sitting in a seat full of petrol almost from the start, and it was actually a relief when the suspension snapped, and he retired. He leapt out of the car and immediately began to tear off his overalls - all in front of a packed grandstand. "The petrol was burning into the most important part of my anatomy and I didn't care what the crowd thought - I just wanted my clothes off," the South African said. Scheckter must have done an impressive job because a local nightclub owner contacted him after a race and offered him $500 for another strip - this time in his club in front of a largely female audience. "He couldn't understand why, when I had done it once that day already for nothing, I wouldn't do it a second time for money...," Scheckter said.

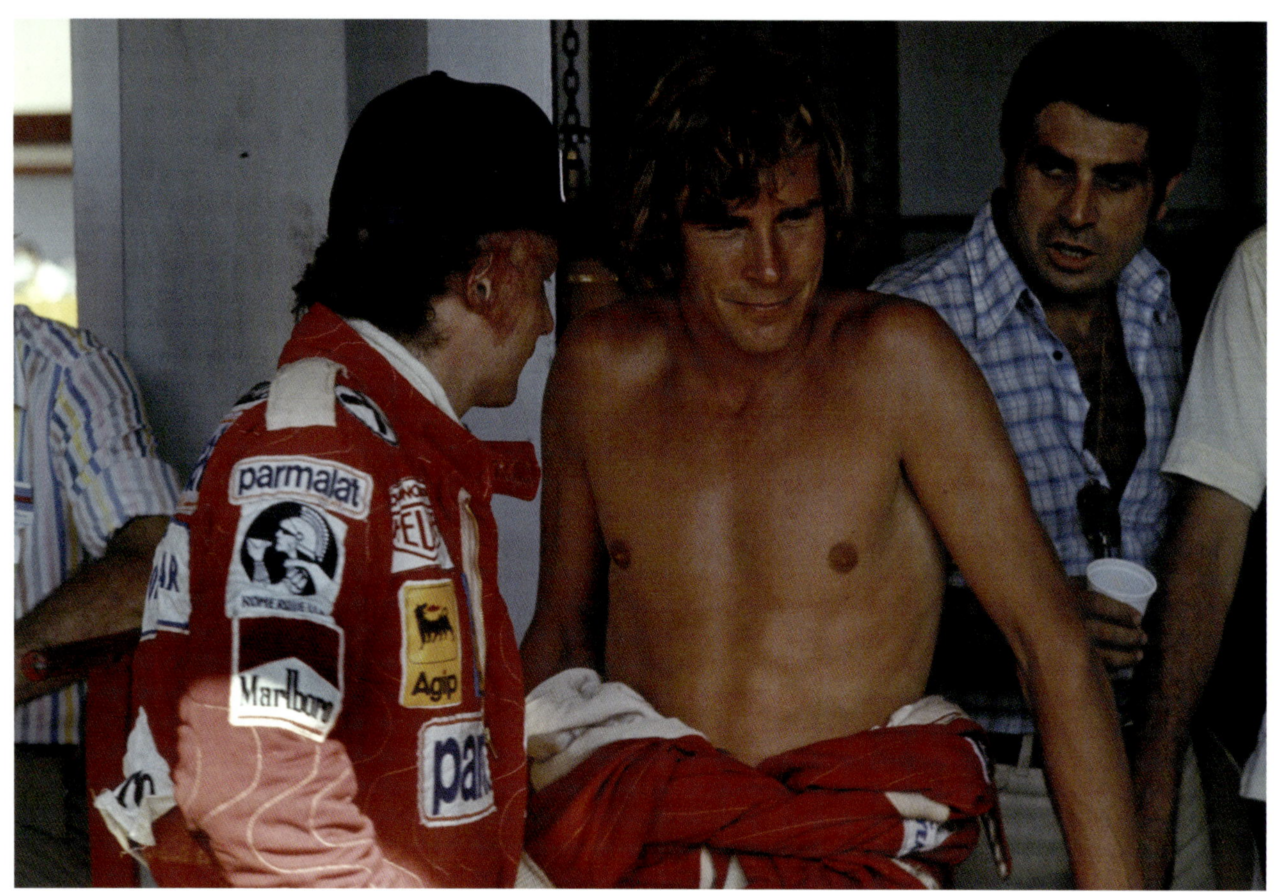

THE WORLD CHAMPION RACES WITH BROKEN RIBS

May 2 1976, Jarama (Spain)

Reigning World Champion Niki Lauda (Ferrari) (photo - left) finished second in the 1976 Spanish Grand Prix, despite breaking two ribs a few days before the race in Jarama. "I had borrowed a tractor to work on the bank by the swimming pool," Lauda said about the accident in his garden in Austria. "The thing tipped over and buried me beneath it. I had the luck to fall between the caterpillar wheels so that I didn't get the whole weight on me. But all the same: My whole right side was done for - broken ribs, blood everywhere, I couldn't get up without help." After two painful weeks Lauda went to Jarama and qualified on the front row. "I don't feel any pain where it is broken because the doctors have killed the nerve," he said after qualifying. "It hurts mostly when I am sliding the car and I can feel the ends of the broken ribs grinding against each other. It must be slowing me down a little bit but I don't know how much." Lauda finished second in the race behind James Hunt (McLaren) but was declared the winner when post-race scrutineering revealed that the McLaren was 180 mm too wide. Hunt was later reinstated and Lauda officially finished second.

POLICE IMPOUND CARS BEFORE PRACTICE

July 30 1976,
Nürburgring (Germany)

RAM, the privateer British team which ran a 'rent-a-racer' operation with a couple of out-dated Brabham BT44s during the 1976 season, had its cars and engines impounded by the German authorities after Friday practice for the German Grand Prix at the Nürburgring. Police officers swooped into the pit garage, where Rolf Stommelen and Lella Lombardi had just left the cars. The police were acting on behalf of Swiss driver Loris Kessel, who had rented one of the team's cars for four races earlier in the season. Kessel claimed there had been a breach of contract and that he was owed 300,000 Deutschmarks by the team. RAM had no option but to withdraw from the rest of the weekend. However, Brabham boss Bernie Ecclestone saved Stommelen by offering him a third works car, and the local hero finished a fine sixth in the race.

42 SECONDS OFF POLE

July 31 1976, Nürburgring (Germany)

Alessandro Pesenti-Rossi was a moderately successful Formula 2 driver, who in 1976 decided it was time to move up to Formula 1. His parents bought him a 1975 Tyrrell-Ford 007 and entered the German Grand Prix at the Nürburgring. The old Nordschleife was not the easiest of circuits on which to make one's F1 debut, and it was no surprise that Pesenti-Rossi qualified last. But that he was exactly 42 seconds slower than James Hunt (McLaren-Ford) on pole position was an eye-opener! He did not qualify for the Dutch Grand Prix, but finished the Austrian and Italian Grands Prix – on both occasions three laps behind the winner. And that was Alessandro Pesenti-Rossi's F1 career, which reportedly cost him £20,000.

A CLOSE SHAVE

August 15 1976
Österreichring (Austria)

Roger Penske has always liked the clean-cut image. His team has enjoyed incredible success in IndyCar, sportscar racing, NASCAR and Trans-Am with immaculately prepared cars, transporters, mechanics. And drivers! When he signed John Watson for his F1 team in late 1975, Penske was less than impressed by the Irishman's somewhat scruffy beard. “I'd had it for a long time, so I said to him: ‘When we win a Grand Prix, I'll shave off my beard,” Watson said. The win – Penske's only in F1 and Wattie's first – came at the 1976 Austrian Grand Prix, and that night Watson duly shaved off his beard. “I went down to breakfast the next morning, and Roger was saying: ‘Where the hell is Watson?’ I replied: ‘Over here, Roger...’ He hadn't recognised me – didn't think I would actually do it.”

HOW DISAPPOINTED CAN YOU BE?

September 12 1976, Monza (Italy)

Austria's Otto Stuppacher was not even close to qualifying his private Tyrrell for the 1976 Italian Grand Prix in Monza – he was almost 14 seconds slower than Jacques Laffite (Ligier-Matra) on pole position. Disappointed not to make his Grand Prix debut, Stuppacher took a flight home to Vienna on Saturday evening. Later that night, the McLarens of James Hunt and Jochen Mass and the Penske of John Watson had their qualifying times disallowed for using illegal fuel, and they were moved to the back of the grid. Suddenly Stuppacher's time was good enough for him to start the race.

But there was more disappointment for the luckless Austrian: there was no way to make it back to Monza in time for the race, so he never officially became a Formula 1 driver.

LOCAL HERO WITH A SHORTCUT

October 24 1976,
Fuji Speedway (Japan)

The 1976 Japanese Grand Prix at Fuji Speedway was a dramatic affair with James Hunt (McLaren) clinching the World Championship after Niki Lauda (Ferrari) decided to withdraw from the very wet race. Local hero Masehiro Hasemi made his F1 debut in the brand new Japanese Kojima, running on locally-made Dunlop tyres. Hasemi was sensationally fast in practice – fourth in the opening session, beaten only by Lauda, Hunt and Carlos Pace (Brabham). He then crashed and could not improve his time, which was still good enough for ninth place on the grid. In the wet-dry race, the Dunlop tyres were not competitive, and Hasemi only finished in a lowly 11th. position. But he was credited with the race's fastest lap even though it later emerged that he had cut part of the circuit, giving him approximately three seconds in hand.

The mistake was never officially corrected, and as Hasemi never returned to F1, he is the only driver in history of F1 to record the fastest lap in what was to be his only race.

FOUR REAR WHEELS BUT TWO-WHEEL-DRIVE

December 1976, Silverstone (Great Britain)

The success of the four-wheeler Tyrrell P34 in 1976 made March designer Robin Herd think. He came to the conclusion that a F1 six-wheeler was actually a good idea – but that it needed four REAR wheels instead of four at the front. In late 1976 he designed the March 2-4-0 with four rear wheels. One of the problems with the Tyrrell P34 was that the small front wheels had to be specially manufactured and developed for the car, but this was not the case with the March 2-4-0 – as all six wheels were regular 1976 Goodyear fronts. The small rear tyres improved the aerodynamics with much 'cleaner' air passing over the rear wing.

And four rear tyres would give strong traction. Too strong, maybe: When March invited the media to the first test of the March 2-4-0 at Silverstone in December, the gearbox – modified from their normal four-wheeler F1 cars - broke after less than half a lap. March team principal (and later FIA president) Max Mosley apologised and asked the journalists back for another test with a stronger gearbox a few days later. But the financially-strained team did not have the resources to develop a proper 4WD gearbox, and what the media saw the following week was a two-wheel-drive six-wheeler with the rearmost wheels no more than jockey wheels with dummy drive shafts. It was a wet day and the driver, Howden Ganley, had been asked not to push too hard – after all, wheel spin from only one set of rear wheels would give away the plot. Still, the car impressed observers, and some even talked about the car's fantastic traction coming out of corners – without any wheel spin! Mosley and the rest of the March management quickly realised that they could not afford to develop the car, and the 2-4-0 was never seen at a Grand Prix.

TOO BIG TO HANDLE

January 9 1977, Buenos Aires (Argentina)

Larry Perkins did not take part in the 1977 Argentina Grand Prix because his BRM was stranded back in England. The BRM P207 looked big and bulky when it was launched in December 1976 and when the team tried to send the car to Buenos Aires, it proved too big to fit through the cargo door of the British Caledonian freighter at Gatwick Airport. With the team, having spent 1976 preparing for their 1977 comeback, only flying the car out to Argentina on the Thursday (the day before official practice kicked off in Buenos Aires), there was no alternative flights and Larry Perkins had to watch the race from the pits

BUSY DAY FOR CLAY

May 19 1977,
Monte Carlo (Monaco

In 1977, the Monaco Grand Prix and final qualifying for the Indy 500 in Indianapolis were held on the same weekend. Clay Regazzoni planned to take part in both races and had it all lined up: with qualifying in Monaco on Thursday and Saturday, he would try to qualify his Ensign-Ford on the Thursday and then fly off to the US and qualify for the Indy 500 before jetting back to Europe for the Monaco Grand Prix on Sunday.

Handling problems with his Ensign meant he was only 21st in the first qualifying session in Monaco and with only the 20 fastest cars allowed to start the race, he decided to stay in Monaco for the final qualifying session. When Saturday dawned wet, suggesting it would be impossible to improve his time from Thursday, he immediately left for Nice and a flight to Indianapolis. He qualified for the Indy 500 – but found out that it had dried out in Monaco and Ensign boss Mo Nunn had offered Regazzoni's car to Belgian veteran Jacky Ickx, who duly qualified for the race, in which he finished 10th. Regazzoni stayed in Indianapolis, started in his first (and only) Indy 500 the following weekend, but retired after just 28 laps.

NO-SHOW FOR DENMARK'S ONLY F1 TEAM

June 19 1977, Anderstorp (Sweden)

F3 driver Jac Nellemann had hired an out-dated Brabham from the RAM team for the 1976 Swedish Grand Prix but he failed to qualify. For 1977 he had more ambitious plans: he bought a 1976 Penske PC3 and created the Grand Prix Racing Denmark team. Nellemann also bought the Ford Cosworth DFV Mario Andretti had used to win the 1976 Japanese Grand Prix for Lotus, and the great Dane's plans embraced several 1977 Grands Prix including his 'local' races in Sweden and Holland. But shortly after Grand Prix Racing Denmark was launched at the annual Auto Show in Copenhagen in January 1977, a national newspaper strike broke out in Denmark. With virtually no media coverage for several weeks, it was impossible to find sponsors for the new team, and shortly before the planned debut in the Swedish Grand Prix, Denmark's first and so far only F1 team closed down.

SABOTAGE!

July 15 1977,
Silverstone (Great Britain)

With 36 drivers entered for the 1977 British Grand Prix, the fight for the 26 places on the starting grid was always going to be tough. A pre-qualifying session on the Wednesday before the race saw six drivers eliminated, but Brian Henton made it through to official practice in his private March. On the night after pre-qualifying, Henton's mechanics locked their pit garage, but when they returned in the morning, the door had been forced open. Close examination suggested that nothing had been removed, and Henton went out for practice and qualifying. He did not qualify - which was probably just as well. When the mechanics stripped down the car a few days later, they found a couple of bearings in the bottom of the gearbox.

The gearbox had been left open overnight after pre-qualifying, but the mysterious bearings did not come from the Henton team. They used a different Hewland gearbox to the other teams with bearings of a different size. "Therefore we can come to no other conclusion than that it was a deliberate attempt at sabotage," Henton's team manager Chris Witty said. "It was just a matter of luck," Witty went on. "Those bearings are quite heavy and the gearbox oil quite thick, and fortunately they remained at the bottom of the gearbox all the time. If they had been picked up and pushed through the cogs, the gearbox would have exploded, and the back wheels would have locked solid. At a place as quick as Silverstone, one can imagine what the consequences might have been..." It was never discovered who had broken into the Henton pit garage and placed the bearings in the gearbox.

ILLEGAL START IN HOME GRAND PRIX

July 31 1977, Hockenheim (Germany):

Local hero Hans Heyer started the 1977 German Grand Prix illegally. The touring car ace was given his first F1 opportunity by the German ATS team but did not qualify for the race. During qualifying, 30 drivers were fighting for the 24 places on the grid and Heyer was only 27th fastest. Still, he used his local knowledge to get into the race. He managed to park his car under the rostrum and waited patiently for the start. "The grid girls were go-kart drivers, and I knew all of them quite well. I told them: 'I have a special job for you: When you walk off the grid, please assemble around my car and try to cover it as much as possible with your signs," Heyer recalls. When the 24 cars qualified for the race had started the race, the grid girls gave the 'all-clear' signal to Heyer. To the delight of the crowd, the German floored the throttle and went off in pursuit of the field. But Hans Heyer's F1 career was all over after nine laps when gear linkage problems forced him to retire. Apparently, Race Control never realised there was one car too many on the track for nine laps, and Heyer was only penalised several weeks later. He was banned for the next F1 races - which he never planned to enter anyway. The 'illegal' 1977 German Grand Prix was his first and last foray into F1. He is the only F1 driver to have been DNQ, DNF and DSQ in the same race.

TO JAPAN AND BACK BUT NO RACE

October 18 1977, Haneda Airport (Japan)

When South African Marsh-Ford driver Ian Scheckter arrived at Tokyo's Haneda Airport a few days before the 1977 Japanese Grand Prix, the local immigration officials were not impressed by the tourist visa in his passport, and because of the country's apartheid regime, professional sportsmen from South Africa were not welcome in Japan. Two police officers escorted Schecker to a nearby hotel, and after 24 hours, he was returned to Europe on the next plane. Just to prove that all men are equal, but some are more equal than others: Ian's brother Jody, winner of the previous race in Canada and second in the World Championship, arrived in Japan without problems and set the fastest lap of the race.

WHEN SPYING WAS LEGAL

December 15 1977, Paul Ricard (France)

'Spying' – or looking very closely at the opposition's cars – is frowned upon in modern Formula 1, and during testing, new cars are kept in the garage behind closed doors or moving curtains. It was not always like that. Just look at this picture from a test session at the Paul Ricard circuit in France in December 1977: Tyrrell had just launched their new 008 car for the 1978 season (it finished in the top-3 in four of the first five races and won in Monaco) and Lotus team principal Colin Chapman was more than a little interested.

A VERY STRANGE STORY

February 12 1978,
Rome (Italy)

On February 12 1978, Giovanna Amati, the 18-year-old daughter of a wealthy cinema owner, was on a date in Rome when she was seized by three masked gunmen. The gang, led by Marseilles gangster Jean Daniel Nieto (31), held her hostage in a wooden cage for 75 days, and she was only released in late April when her father met the kidnappers' demand of almost $1 million (reportedly the box office receipts from the first Star Wars film in the family's almost 50 cinemas in and around Rome).

It was claimed that Nieto had fallen in love with Miss Amati during her captivity, and the Italian media reported that bouquets of red roses and love letters began to arrive at the family home shortly after her release. In late May, Giovanna agreed to meet her kidnapper again, and the police followed her to the meeting place in Rome's elegant Via Veneto. After a wild shootout amid the cafes, Nieto was arrested and later sentenced to 18 years in prison. A couple of years later, Giovanna Amati attended a motor racing school with her friend Elio de Angelis, and she made her debut in Formula Abarth in 1981. She progressed to Formula 3 and from 1987 she took part in the International Formula 3000 Championship. Four years in Formula 3000 produced a modest seventh place as her best result, but for 1992 she signed for the Brabham Formula 1 team. She did not qualify for the three opening races of the season in South Africa, Mexico and Brazil and was replaced by Damon Hill (who qualified for only two of the next eight races). Giovanna Amati is still the last woman to attempt to qualify for a Formula 1 Grand Prix.

SPIES LIKE US

July 31 1978,
London High Court (Great Britain)

In late 1977, most of the leading members of the Shadow team – including business manager Jackie Oliver, team manager Alan Rees and technical director Tony Southgate – broke away and created their own Arrows team for 1978. When Shadow and Arrows launched their 1978 cars, they were not only similar – they were virtually identical. Shadow took Arrows to court, accusing Southgate and Co. of infringing their copyright – implying the drawings made for the 1978 Shadow in late 1977 were also used for the Arrows. The High Court in London agreed – Mr Justice Templeman ruling that 40% of the components in the Arrows had been copied from the Shadow drawings. With immediate effect, the Arrows was banned from racing, but Jackie Oliver and his crew had anticipated that they would lose the case. In just 52 days, a brand new – and original - Arrows was designed and built so the team didn't miss a race.

WORK IN PROGRESS ON THE M23

September 10 1978, Monza (Italy)

Nelson Piquet's ninth place in the 1978 Italian Grand Prix was the final chapter in the history of one of the longest-serving F1 cars. The Brazilian was driving a McLaren M23 (photo), a model which had made its debut in the South African Grand Prix more than five years earlier. The Ford Cosworth DFV-powered car won the 1974 and 1976 World Championships with Emerson Fittipaldi and James Hunt behind the wheel. The McLaren works team introduced the M26 in late 1976, and it gradually replaced the M23 during 1977. But the M23 was still used by private teams until its swansong with Piquet in 1978. In total, the McLaren M23 took part in 80 Grands Prix between 1973 and 1978 and winning 16 of them, taking 14 pole positions and setting 10 fastest laps.

STARS BAN YOUNG RIVAL

October 1 1978,
Watkins Glen (United States)

In 1978 Riccardo Patrese was a young man in a hurry. In South Africa, he came within 15 laps of winning the new Arrows team's second Grand Prix and he finished second in the Swedish Grand Prix, ahead of local hero Ronnie Peterson. Patrese was quick but erratic and he had a few accidents. When the popular Peterson died after a multi-car accident at the start of the Italian Grand Prix at Monza, many of the established drivers lashed out to find a scapegoat.
The young Italian had made another aggressive start, and several of his older colleagues accused him of causing the accident. "Without warning, Patrese barged over on me, pushing me into Ronnie," 1976 World Champion James Hunt said.
"He drives with a complete disregard for anyone else on the track," John Watson added. The leading drivers got together and sent an ultimatum to the organisers of the next race, the United States Grand Prix in Watkins Glen (photo): "If you let Patrese race, we will not take part." The organisers at Watkins Glen duly turned down Patrese's entry. Patrese insisted that he did not cause the accident, and the Italian was subsequently officially cleared of any responsibility for the tragedy in Monza. The following week Patrese returned to Formula 1 in the Canadian Grand Prix. He matured into one of the safest and most respected drivers in the history of the sport. When he retired after the 1993 season, he had driven more Grands Prix than anybody else.

COLD IN CANADA

October 8 1978, Montreal (Canada)

In 1978, the Canadian Grand Prix moved from Mosport Park near Toronto to the man-made Île Notre-Dame, in the middle of the St. Lawrence river in Montreal. It turned out to be a wet weekend with rain affecting both Friday and Saturday. Sunday was mostly cloudy and cold: the official weather statistics for the Montreal area reported temperatures of only 5 degrees C, making the race the coldest in Formula 1 history. For the record, local hero Gilles Villeneuve (Ferrari- photo) won the race ahead of Jody Scheck-ter (Wolf-Ford) and Carlos Reutemann (Ferrari).

THE LEAST SUCCESSFUL TEAM EVER?

May 12 1979, Zolder (Belgium)

Willy Kauhsen, who was the 1967 European Touring Car Champion and runner-up in the 1970 Le Mans 24 Hours, founded his own racing team in 1976. Two seasons of Formula 2 brought little success, but despite this he decided to enter Formula 1. He spent 1978 building a 'kit car' with a chassis designed in-house, a Ford Cosworth DFV engine and a Hewland gearbox. This was tested by Belgian Patrick Neve at Paul Ricard (photo). The small team did not take part in the early fly-away races in 1979 in Argentina, Brazil, South Africa and at Long Beach, but Kauhsen was ready for the Spanish Grand Prix in Jarama, the first European round. The Kauhsen WK was driven by Italy's Gianfranco Brancatelli but failed to qualify with the Italian's best lap almost nine seconds slower than Jacques Laffite's (Ligier-Ford) pole position time. Two weeks later Brancatelli – this time more than 13 seconds slower than Laffite's pole – again failed to qualify. That was the end of the Kauhsen F1 Team – Willy Kauhsen withdrew from Formula 1 and closed the team. Most of the assets were sold to Italy's Arturo Merzario, who ran his own operation. The Kauhsen was rebuilt and renamed the Merzario A4 – which then failed to qualify for the seven rounds it was entered for in the second half of the season.

FORMEL 1
GRAND PRIX OF SWEDEN
ANDERSTORP
14-16 JUNI 1979
World Championship of Drivers
SCANDINAVIAN RACEWAY

THE RACE THAT NEVER WAS

June 16 1979, Anderstorp (Sweden)

Sweden was a superpower in Formula 1 in the mid-1970s. The Nordic country had two race winners in the field with Ronnie Peterson and Gunnar Nilsson and they had a Grand Prix in Anderstorp. But things went downhill in late 1978. Peterson was killed in a tragic accident in the Italian Grand Prix in Monza and Nilsson succumbed to cancer a few weeks later. The loss of Peterson and Nilsson led to a reaction against motor sport in Sweden, and a month before the 1979 Grand Prix, the race sponsor pulled out.

The demand for tickets had also dropped dramatically, and the organisers in Anderstorp did not have the 2.2 million Swedish Kroner (app. €300,000) for the guarantee demanded by the Formula One Constructors Association. The race, scheduled for June 16, was officially cancelled on May 16. A few days later a new sponsor suddenly appeared on the scene. For a couple of days in mid May, the race was 'on' again, but on May 21 the FIA finally announced that the Swedish Grand Prix would not take place. "This decision has been taken as the organisers found it impossible to provide the necessary guarantee four weeks before the race." That was the end of the Swedish Grand Prix – and of Sweden's time as a F1 superpower.

WHEN ENOUGH IS ENOUGH

September 28 1979, Montreal (Canada)

During the opening practice session for the 1979 Canadian Grand Prix on the Île Notre Dame circuit in Montreal, Niki Lauda suddenly decided he'd had enough. He had won two World Championships in 1975 and 1977 for Ferrari, almost lost his life in a dramatic accident in the German Grand Prix 1976 and spent 1978 and 1979 with Bernie Ecclestone's Brabham team. He returned to the pits and informed a surprised Ecclestone (right) that he had quit racing with immediate effect. "The thought came to me as I turned into one of the corners: I no longer want to drive a racing car round in circles," he explained. Lauda returned to his hotel in downtown Montreal and then went to the airport and left Canada. Ecclestone quickly put Argentina's Ricardo Zunino in Lauda's car, but it was not all over for the Austrian: Two years later he returned to Formula 1 with McLaren and won the 1984 title before retiring for the second and final time at the end of 1985.

80's

ONCE BITTEN, TWICE SHY

February 28 1980, Kyalami (South Africa)

Marc Surer and South Africa's Kyalami circuit were not a good match. In practice for the 1980 South African Grand Prix, Surer crashed his ATS (photo), and was put in hospital with two broken ankles. Four months later, he made his comeback in the French Grand Prix, and he raced for Ensign the following year.

He got his big chance when he signed with Arrows for 1982. On Friday January 15 he took part in a private test in preparation for the opening Grand Prix of the year in Kyalami the following weekend. It is thought that a broken rear rocker arm sent the Arrows straight into the barrier. Surer probably knew what was coming: two broken feet. Once again, the brave Swiss fought his way back to racing, making his comeback in the Belgian Grand Prix four months later.

WORLD CHAMPION KNOCKS DOWN VIP GUEST

March 1 1980,
Kyalami (South Africa)

Alan Jones was not happy after retiring from the 1980 South African Grand Prix. And his mood didn't improve when team principal Frank Williams asked him to go down to a tent of one of their sponsors to shake hands and sign autographs. Things went from bad to worse for the Australian when a somewhat intoxicated guest came up to him and said: “Hey boy – you blew your car up, eh?” In Jones's own words, he “whacked him a couple”, and the VIP guest went to the floor. Jones left, and when he woke up the next day, he was obviously worried about the incident until he saw a newspaper: ‘Drunk Attacks Sportsman in Hospitality Tent’.“It wasn't quite like that, but it saved us all embarrassment,” he said. Jones won the World Championship that year.

HORSE POWER

June 29 1980,
Paul Ricard (France)

Alan Jones was somewhat surprised when a horse appeared during the podium ceremony after the 1980 French Grand Prix (photo). "I thought: 'That's funny'," he explained later. "Then they asked me if I would sit on it." Later, when Alan was relaxing in the Williams motorhome, a man arrived and asked where he would like to have his horse tied up.
Jones, thinking the visitor was joking, said: "Just tie it to the bumper." When he eventually emerged from the motorhome, there was a horse tied to the motorhome. It was actually Jones's prize for winning the race. "I had to ship it from Marseilles to Holland, then from Holland to London and eventually back to Australia," he said. "It did a few kilometres, that horse!"

WHERE IS MY PIT-CREW?

August 17 1980, Österreichring (Austria)

Bruno Giacomelli was in great form in the 1980 Austrian Grand Prix. From eighth place on the grid, he made a strong start in his Alfa Romeo, and was running fourth in the opening stages. The heavy Alfa Romeo was hard on its rear tyres, and at the end of the 28th lap, he came into the pits for fresh rubber. The Alfa Romeo mechanics were all on the pit wall, waiting for their car to pass on the track. Only when he had blipped the V12 engine several times to attract attention, did the Alfa Romeo mechanics realise that Giacomelli was behind them in the pit-lane, waiting to have his tyres changed.

TWO WORLD CHAMPIONSHIPS FOR 1981

October 31 1980, London (Great Britain)

A civil war broke out in Formula 1 in the autumn of 1980, when the majority of the teams could not agree with the FIA about regulations and commercial arrangements. On October 31, it was announced that there would be two World Championships the following year. FIA would continue with their original series, which only had the manufacturer teams from Ferrari, Renault and Alfa Romeo on the entry list. But a new rival series organised by the Formula One Constructors Association (FOCA) and its president Bernie Ecclestone would also take place.

A new organisation the World Federation of Motor Sport/WFMS - was set up specifically to run the new FOCA series, officially titled 'The World Professional Drivers Championship' and officially launched in Paris (photo). With entries from 11 teams including McLaren, Williams, Ligier, Lotus and Brabham, the FOCA series had a full grid, and they announced a 1981 calendar with 18 races (including a Grand Prix in New York on May 2). The first of the WFMS races was scheduled to take place on the Kyalami circuit in South Africa on February 7. Work on a peace deal continued through the winter, and FOCA eventually agreed to drop the WFMS idea. A compromise, which saw FOCA and Ecclestone take over most of the commercial matters while FIA remained in charge of the regulations, was reached so late that the race in Kyalami took place. The FOCA teams put on a great show with Carlos Reutemann winning for Williams. The Kyalami race was run not part of the FIA series and consequently did not count for the World Championship, which kicked off a few weeks later with Alfa Romeo, Ferrari and Renault joining the FOCA teams in Long Beach. And no, the FIA Formula 1 World Championship 1981 did not include a race in New York...

SPEED IS A DRUG

March 5 1981
Jacarepagua (Brazil)

An unofficial test session was organised on the Wednesday before the 1981 Brazilian Grand Prix at the Jacarepagua circuit outside Rio de Janeiro. The driver of the Ensign team's sole entry was a surprise: Ricardo Londono, a man with little experience and no Superlicence. He was not the obvious choice for the small team.

Or perhaps he was: the Columbian could provide some much-needed money for the financially hard-pressed team. The problem was that it was suggested that the money came from drug trafficking.

The rumours gathered pace when Londono was accompanied in the paddock by some serious looking types - three of whom had featured on the cover of an American magazine as among the most wanted men in the world! Still, Londono impressed in the uncompetitive car and looked on his way to securing the Superlicence when he had a small collision with Keke Rosberg (Fittipaldi-Ford). With more and more people realising that the connection between Londono, his sinister friends, dubious money and Formula 1 was not a great idea, the Rosberg incident became the official explanation why Londono was refused a Superlicence. Thus, the Jacarepagua test session was both the beginning and the end of Ricardo Londono's F1 career. Later he began to sell aircrafts, boats and helicopters in his home country – more often than not to recognised drug dealers.

In 2000 the Columbian authorities seized most of Londono's $10 million fortune, claiming it came from drug trafficking. Nine years later, in June 2009, Londono and his two bodyguards were assassinated. The background to the murder? In local media, it was attributed to 'differences with another drug baron'.

RACING WITH ABBA

May 3 15 1981,
Imola (Italy)

The name on the ATS-Ford in the 1981 San Marino Grand Prix was both unusual and famous: What was ABBA, the Swedish pop group who had just released their seventh album 'Super Trouper', doing in Formula 1? Swedish F3 driver Slim Borgudd was also an accomplished drummer, and he had taken part in recording sessions with ABBA. When ATS was looking for a new driver after team principal Günther Schmid had fallen out with Holland's Jan Lammers, Borgudd stepped up, complete with ABBA's logo for the sidepods. It was not a sponsorship as such – more a goodwill gesture from the Swedish supergroup, which would attract more conventional sponsors to the team. It was also not a case of 'The Winner Takes It All' (one of the hit singles from 'Super Trouper'), but Borgudd still took a fine sixth place and one World Championship point in the British Grand Prix (photo) a few weeks later.

ARNOUX SPENDS RACE DAY IN PRISON

May 16 1981, Zolder (Belgium)

While the Belgian Grand Prix took place at the Zolder circuit, Renault driver Rene Arnoux spent the day in a nearby gaol. Car problems during Friday's qualifying session and rain on Saturday meant the Frenchman failed to qualify for the race, and when he left the circuit on Saturday evening, he found himself in a traffic jam. He pulled out and passed a few cars and slotted into a gap further up the line. The driver of the car behind Arnoux was not impressed, got out of his car – and jumped onto the bonnet of Arnoux's Renault 5! When he refused to get off, the Renault driver set off to the hotel, reportedly hitting 70 km/h on the way with his passenger clinging to the windscreen wipers. At the hotel, some five kilometres from the circuit, Arnoux's new 'friend' called the police, and the Renault driver was arrested and spent race day in prison.

MECHANIC'S MIRACULOUS ESCAPE ON GRID

May 17 1981, Zolder (Belgium)

The start of the 1981 Belgian Grand Prix was chaotic. Many drivers felt the organisers and the FIA ignored their demands for a limited number of cars on the track and in the pits during qualifying and decided to stage a protest on the grid. On live TV, drivers left their cars and walked to the front of the grid. This delayed the start, and when the drivers had returned to their cars, the final parade lap was a confused business. Riccardo Patrese stalled his Arrows on the grid and waved his arms. His chief mechanic Dave Luckett, believing there would be another warm-up lap, jumped over the barrier with a battery to restart the car. At that very moment, with Luckett crouching behind Patrese's car, the race started. Several drivers avoided Luckett and the stricken car, but Patrese's team-mate Siegfried Stohr ran into it - with Luckett trapped between the Arrows cars. Miraculously, he escaped with a broken leg and rib, two broken fingers and light concussion.

DRY RACE DELAYED BY WET TRACK

May 31 1981, Monte Carlo (Monaco)

The 1981 Monaco Grand Prix had a late start at 15.30, so that Prince Rainier could finish his lunch. The long wait in glorious sunshine was suddenly interrupted by sirens as fire engines and ambulances rushed to the Hotel Loews, above the circuit's famous tunnel. A fire had broken out in the hotel kitchen. This was extinguished by firemen, using hundreds of gallons of water... which leaked through the floor and began to cascade into the tunnel. Bernie Ecclestone and the president of the Grand Prix Drivers Association (GPDA) Jody Scheckter inspected the wet tunnel, and the start was delayed and there was even talk of cancelling the race. In the end the race started almost an hour late with a yellow flag zone from before the tunnel down to the chicane. Gilles Villeneuve (photo) took his Ferrari to a great win in Formula 1's only dry race with a 'wet zone'.

TOP-13 WITH 13 DIFFERENT CARS

July 18 1981,
Silverstone (Great Britain)

Seventeen teams took part in the 1981 Formula One World Championship and the British Grand Prix produced an amazing result with the top 13 finishers all coming from different teams! John Watson (photo) won for McLaren ahead of Carlos Reutemann (Williams) and Jacques Laffite (Talbot-Ligier). The remaining 10 teams in the top-13 were Tyrrell, Brabham, ATS, March, Osella, Renault, Arrows, Theodore, Alfa Romeo and Fittipaldi.

“HEROIN? IT'S MY PAYMENT FROM MI5!”

August 17 1981, London (Great Britain)

On Monday August 17 1981, The Times newspaper reported that “a company consultant will appear before Bow Street Magistrates charged with possessing heroin worth about £1 million.” His name was Ian Burgess – and he was a former F1 driver. Burgess, who had been an office manager at the Cooper factory, made his debut in the Formula 1 World Championship in a works-Cooper in the 1959 British Grand Prix. He did several races for the Centro Sud team in 1959 and 1960, scoring his best result with a sixth place in the 1959 German Grand Prix. His career in the Formula 1 World Championship came to an end with two races for the American Scirocco-Powell team in 1963 (photo). He was out of the spotlight until his arrest carrying a large quantity of heroin when he was passing through British customs. He explained that this had been given to him by MI5, as payment for intelligence work in the Middle East. MI5 declined to confirm this unlikely story, which is hardly surprising as it is Britain’s secret security service, tasked with protecting the country, and its work is generally done in Britain, while MI6 is the Secret Intelligence Service, which gathers information around the world.

The judge did not believe the story and Burgess was sent to prison for 10 years. Legend has it that after a while he was transferred to Ford Open Prison in West Sussex and one day quietly departed, met a Czech girlfriend, who was waiting for him and disappeared off to Czechoslovakia, which was still behind the Iron Curtain in those days. He reappeared in Spain and would make low profile visits to Britain from time to time. He eventually returned to London and died in Harrow in 2012, at the age of 81.

GRASS STRIP IN THE PITS

September 26 1981, Montreal (Canada)

Friday practice for the 1981 Canadian Grand Prix on the Île Notre Dame in Montreal took place under blue skies and in bright sunshine, but on their way out on the circuit, the drivers had an unusual distraction. On the grass strip between the pit lane and the pit wall across from the Alfa Romeo garage, a local beauty decided to enjoy the autumn sun in her bikini. Nobody knew where she came from, but it was very clear she did not have a pit lane credential on her. Nobody seemed to care, and the drivers probably enjoyed the sight. When Saturday was overcast and it rained on Sunday, the bikini babe was not seen again.

WITH FRIENDS LIKE THIS...

October 17 1981, Las Vegas (United States)

1981 Williams drivers Alan Jones and Carlos Reutemann were not the best of friends. The Argentine ignored team orders early in the season, and Jones was furious, but he got his revenge in the final race of the year, the Caesars Palace Grand Prix in Las Vegas. By then, Jones had lost all chance of winning the World Championship, but Reutemann was fighting Nelson Piquet (Brabham) for the title.

The two Williams drivers qualified first and second with Reutemann fastest, and now Jones played his little trick. He told his teammate: "Have you seen where the pole is? It's just a disgrace – there is shit everywhere. I don't know how you're going to get off the line," he said to Reutemann. At the time, the fastest man in qualifying would decide where pole position was, and following Jones's advice, Reutemann went to the organisers and told them he wanted the pole on the other side of the grid. Jones just laughed – "I got pole thanks to my mouth," he said later. Jones ran down the dirty side on every lap during the Sunday morning warm-up session, to clean it up, and when the race started, he easily out-dragged Reutemann off the grid (photo). Jones went on the win the race – and Reutemann lost the title to Piquet.

DRIVERS ON STRIKE – SPEND THE NIGHT IN DORMITORY

January 21 1982, Johannesburg (South Africa)

The Grand Prix Drivers Association was not happy with new rules about their Superlicences introduced shortly before the 1982 season. When negotiations with the FIA failed to solve the problem, GPDA leader and Ferrari driver Didier Pironi invited all the drivers to a meeting a couple of hours before practice for the first Grand Prix of the season in Kyalami. But instead of having the meeting at the circuit, Pironi ushered the drivers to a bus, which left for a conference room at the Sunnyside Park Hotel in Johannesburg, 40 minutes away. Pironi and McLaren driver Niki Lauda, who was making his comeback to F1 after two years away from the sport, considered it paramount that the drivers stayed together away from pressure from their team bosses and the FIA. During the day, a couple of team principals tried to enter the conference room, but the drivers barricaded the door. Pironi returned to Kyalami to negotiate with FIA, while the drivers at the hotel enjoyed their new-found camaraderie (photo: Riccardo Paletti/ Osella-Ford - left, Rene Arnoux/Renault - centre and Mauro Baldi/ Arrows-Ford - right on balcony). Gilles Villeneuve (Ferrari) and Elio de Angelis (Lotus) entertained their colleagues with their piano-playing skills. When no solution was found, a dormitory was set up with mattresses on the floor and two or even three drivers sharing a bed. Negotiations between the FIA, Pironi and Lauda continued on Friday morning, and a compromise was finally reached. It was not the end of the problem, which was only solved later in the year, but it allowed qualifying on Friday afternoon and the South African Grand Prix the following day to go ahead.

WHEN TWO IS (NOT) TWICE AS GOOD

April 4 1982,
Long Beach (United States)

There was instant controversy when Ferrari rolled out its cars for Gilles Villeneuve and Didier Pironi for Saturday practice at the 1982 United States West Grand Prix in Long Beach. Both cars featured a 'twin' rear wing – actually two wings bolted together, one in front of the other. At a time when the maximum width of the rear wing was 110 cm, the total width of the 'twin' wing, which extended almost to the edge of the rear wheels, was close to 200 cm. Ferrari argued that each individual wing was legal and that there was nothing in the rules which limited the number of wings. This did not convince the stewards. While Pironi was an early retirement, Villeneuve was disqualified from third place after the race.

MOST TEAMS STAY AWAY

April 25 1982, Imola (Italy)

The Formula 1 field in 1982 was split up into two groups: the 'Grandees' – factory teams like Ferrari and Renault, which ran with heavy, powerful turbo engines; and the 'Garagistes' – mostly British teams, which ran with the old, reliable but under-powered normally aspirated Ford Cosworth V8s. The 'Garagistes' had a hard time fighting the superior turbo engines but came up with a clever idea. The rules defined the cars' minimum weight as the 'weight of the car in running order with its normal quantity of lubricants and coolants, but without any fuel or driver aboard'. In other words – topping up the oil tank and brake coolant reservoir to 'normal levels' was allowed before the post-race scrutineering. With their light Cosworth engines, the 'Garagistes' could easily build cars under the 580 kg minimum weight, and at the Brazilian Grand Prix, many cars appeared with big water bags - supposedly to cool the brakes. The trick was to jettison the water early in the race, run underweight for most of the distance, and top up the water bag again before scrutineering. When Nelson Piquet (Brabham) and Keke Rosberg (Williams) finished first and second in Brazil in 'water-cooled' cars, Renault made an official protest. It was rejected by the stewards in Brazil, but Renault appealed to the FIA, which duly disqualified both drivers. Another loophole in the F1 rules had been closed. The row didn't stop there: most of the 'Garagistes' claimed that they did not have sufficient time to redesign their cars for the 'new rules' and stayed away from the first race after the appeal court's decision. Thus the 1982 San Marino Grand Prix was held with only 14 cars on the grid (photo).

ANYBODY WANT TO WIN THIS RACE?

May 23 1982, Monte Carlo (Monaco)

The closing laps of the 1982 Monaco were among the most dramatic and perplexing in the history of the Formula 1 World Championship. Drizzle had made the track slippery, but three laps from the end, Alain Prost (Renault) seemed to be in a secure lead. Then the Frenchman lost control and crashed into the barrier. With Prost out, Riccardo Patrese (Brabham-Ford - photo) took over the lead – for a few hundred metres - but the Italian then spun and stalled at the Loews hairpin. That put Didier Pironi (Ferrari), minus its nose, into the lead, but he stopped halfway round the final lap with electrical problems. Andrea de Cesaris inherited the lead for a few seconds – until his Alfa Romeo ran out of fuel. Derek Daly, who had lost his rear wing earlier, was then deemed to be leading but he hit the wall in the Swimming Pool area and retired. The official waiting at the finish line with the chequered flag was as confused as everybody else as nobody appeared for a long time. Finally, Patrese, who had managed to restart his Brabham, arrived to win the race – the only driver to complete the full race distance of 76 laps.

FIGHTING ON BOTH FRONTS

September 12 1982, Monza (Italy

The 1978 World Champion Mario Andretti had retired from Formula 1 after the 1981 season. But when Carlos Reutemann suddenly quit the Williams team in early 1982, the American was called in to replace him in the United States Grand Prix West in Long Beach. He retired from the race, and that seemed like the end of a great F1 career. But when Ferrari's Didier Pironi was seriously injured in practice for the German Grand Prix, Andretti made another comeback – this time for the Prancing Horse. He put the Ferrari on pole position for the Italian Grand Prix in Monza (photo) and finished in a fine third place. Andretti also drove for Ferrari in the final race of the year, the Las Vegas Grand Prix. While Andretti's Williams team-mate in Long Beach, Finland's Keke Rosberg, went on to win the 1982 Drivers' World Championship, the American's third place in Monza helped Ferrari clinch the Constructors' title.

WORLD CHAMPION AFTER ONE WIN

September 25 1982, Las Vegas (United States)

When Keke Rosberg (Williams-Ford) crossed the line in the 1982 Caesars Palace Grand Prix in Las Vegas in fifth place, it was enough to clinch the 1982 World Championship. Even more remarkable was the fact the Finn had only won one Grand Prix in his F1 career! Rosberg had won the Swiss Grand Prix in Dijon earlier that year, but in a season with 11 different winners, consistency was paramount, and the Finn scored points in 10 of the 15 races. Keke Rosberg, father of 2016 World Champion Nico, went on to win another four Grands Prix before he retired from F1 in 1986. With only one win, Keke Rosberg took the 1982 World Championship after winning 6.6% of the races. Max Verstappen (Red Bull-Honda) took the 2023 title by winning 19 of the 22 races – that is a staggering 86.4%!

DISQUALIFIED FOR RACING A DIFFERENT TYPE OF CAR

March 13 1983,
Rio de Janeiro (Brazil)

After 16 years with the normally-aspirated Ford Cosworth V8 engine, Lotus would make the switch for Renault's turbocharged V6 engine in 1983. But Renault did not have a sufficient number of engines available, and while Elio de Angelis (photo) was destined to start the season with Renault engines, his teammate Nigel Mansell would remain Ford powered until mid-season. Lotus's Renault collaboration started badly when the engine in de Angelis's car began to smoke during the warm-up lap before the opening race in Brazil. The Italian was quickly crammed into the spare car – which had a Ford Cosworth engine. De Angelis went on to finish 13th in the race but was later disqualified. While it was OK to take the spare car in those days, it was not allowed to race in a different type of car. And a Lotus-Ford was definitely different from a Lotus-Renault.

MY TEAM, MY RULES

March 24 1984, Jacarepagua (Brazil)

Günther Schmid (with headset), the owner of the ATS team, was never an easy man to work with. Shortly before the first race of the 1984 season, the Brazilian Grand Prix in Rio de Janeiro, team manager Paul Owens was fired. Some technical staff had also left the team at short notice, so Schmidt decided to run the show himself, acting as both team manager and engineer. Neither job was among Schmid's main competences, and things went from bad to worse when his driver Manfred Winkelhock ran out of fuel on his way into the pits during qualifying. Schmid ordered his mechanics to push the car back to the ATS pits. On the way, they ignored the demands of the FIA marshals to go into the weigh-in area with the car, and Schmid was called in front of the stewards to explain the 'misunderstanding'. During the interview, the temperamental German was not... shall we say: very tactful. The result: Winkelhock was disqualified for the rest of the weekend.

BROTHERS IN ARMS

March 25 1984,
Jacarepagua (Brazil)

Teo Fabi had a problem in early 1984. After a less than successful F1 debut in 1982 with the uncompetitive Toleman-Hart, he had spent 1983 in the American CART-series with the Forsythe team, winning three races and finishing second in the championship. He re-signed with Forsythe for 1984, but then came the problem: Brabham team owner Bernie Ecclestone offered him a F1 contract for 1984 alongside reigning World Champion Nelson Piquet. It was too good to resist, and a solution was found. Teo would drive the Brabham (photo) whenever the F1 schedule did not clash with his CART commitments – and when he was busy in the States, his younger brother Corrado would take over the Brabham. Teo thus raced in the first five Grands Prix of the year before Corrado took over in Monaco and Canada, when the older Fabi was busy in Milwaukee and Portland. Teo then returned for the Detroit Grand Prix (finishing a fine third) but Corrado was back in the Brabham for the Dallas Grand Prix two weeks later. And then the penny dropped: the constant change of cars and drivers was not really helping Brabham, Forsythe or the Fabi brothers. For the rest of the year, Corrado raced the Forsythe car in the CART series while Teo focussed full-time on his F1 commitments with Bernie E and Brabham.

AND THE CIRCUIT IS...?

June 2 1984, Monte Carlo (Monaco)

With 27 cars present and only 20 allowed to start the race, qualifying for the 1984 Monaco Grand Prix was dramatic. The few cars with normally aspirated engines, which were at least 150 bhp down on their turbo charged rivals, were really up against the wall. And Martin Brundle in his Tyrrell-Ford (photo) in more ways than one: on his fastest lap, his brakes failed going into the Tabac corner, and he went straight into the barrier. The Tyrrell was flipped onto its side and skated down the track. "The car was still on its side when they got me out. My instinct told me to get back to the pits for the spare car," Brundle said. The crowd cheered when the Englishman ran back to the pits and climbed into the spare Tyrrell. It was only when he sat in the car and waited for the green light, he felt the after-effects of the crash. When team boss Ken Tyrrell informed him that there were only eight minutes of qualifying remaining and that he was currently in 22nd. position, Brundle replied: "Yes – not a problem. But – which track am I at? Do I turn right or left when I get to the end of the pit lane?" Ken Tyrrell didn't even reply – he simply reached into the cockpit and turned off the engine. No Monaco Grand Prix for Martin Brundle...

LET'S WATER THE TUNNEL

June 3 1984, Monte Carlo (Monaco)

The start of the very wet 1984 Monaco Grand Prix was delayed by 15 minutes because the local firemen had to spray water onto the track in the tunnel under the Loews Hotel. In the morning warm-up, water carried into the tunnel from the rain tyres on the cars had made the tunnel section more slippery than the rest of the circuit. According to Williams-Honda driver Keke Rosberg, the combination of grease and water made it more slippery than anything else he had known. To remove some of the grease and to make the track 'uniformly wet', fire hoses were put to use in the tunnel before the start.

FASTEST LAP FROM SUPPORT RACE

July 8 1984,
Dallas (United States)

The first and only Grand Prix on the street circuit in Dallas's Fair Park in July 1984 (photo) was a bizarre affair. To begin with, it was a hot weekend in Texas – temperatures soared into the 40s and at one stage, track temperatures of 66 degrees Celsius were recorded. When Osella's Piercarlo Ghinzani pitted for fresh tyres, he was completely finished, but the mechanics revived him by emptying a bucket of cold water into the cockpit. Nigel Mansell's Lotus stopped within sight of the chequered flag, and the brave Englishman tried to push the car across the line – only to collapse dramatically due to dehydration and exhaustion. The track surface began to crumble soon after practice started on Friday, and emergency repairs with quick drying cement shortly before the start did not solve the problem. The cement failed to cure in the Texan heat.

Towards the end of the race, the track was more suited to rallycross than Formula 1, and the fastest lap, set by Niki Lauda's McLaren-TAG, was actually slower than the fastest lap of the supporting CanAm sports car race held on the Saturday, when the track was in a marginally better condition. Keke Rosberg won the race in a Williams-Honda, but even before the start, he summed up the Dallas Grand Prix: "What a joke!"

"FP2? THAT'S IN 105 DAYS"

September 14 1985, Spa-Francorchamps (Belgium)

These days, there are 2.5 hours between the FP1 and FP2 practice sessions on Fridays. At the 1985 Belgian Grand Prix, there were...105 days. FP1 started as scheduled on Friday morning May 31st at 10.00 with Michele Alboreto (Ferrari) topping the time sheets. But the track was crumbling – it had been resurfaced only a few days earlier, and the tarmac was clearly not ready for the fat, grippy F1 rear tyres. The second session was stopped, the drivers inspected the track (photo) and no times were officially recorded. On Friday night, the Belgian organisers tried to repair the damage with yet another new layer of asphalt on the trouble spots, but it didn't really help, and the Belgian Grand Prix was postponed until September 15. It was bad news for the spectators – and it was bad news for the new Beatrice Haas-team, which made its F1 debut in the Italian Grand Prix on September 8. It had not been entered in the original race in the spring and was not allowed to take part when the second part of the 1985 Belgian Grand Prix kicked off with FP2 on Friday September 13 – some 105 days after FP1.

THE MYSTERIOUS CASE OF BAP ROMANO

November 3 1985, Adelaide (Australia)

The first Australian Formula 1 Grand Prix was held in Adelaide in early November 1985. The field consisted of 25 cars including Australia's own 1980 World Champion Alan Jones (in a Beatrice-Ford). But there could have been another local hero in the race: Bap Romano, who had finished sixth in the 1985 Australian Sports Car Championship in his own Cosworth powered Romano WE84, claimed he had come to an arrangement with the Tyrrell team to race a Tyrrell-Ford Cosworth alongside regular drivers Martin Brundle and Ivan Capelli, who had Tyrrell-Renaults. According to the Romano Group website, "Ken Tyrrell (photo) confirmed the payment figure to run the Cosworth car", and the brewery divisions of the Bond Corporation offered sponsorship in excess of three and a half times the payment figure required by the Tyrrell organization. The only other requirement was that CAMS had to endorse Romano's nomination to drive the car. And that, apparently, was a problem. CAMS did not support Romano's request for a Superlicence – according to the Romano Group website because "CAMS did not want to have an accident on their first Grand Prix." And this is where the less-than-illustrious F1 career of the mysterious Bap Romano ended.

RUNNING ON EMPTY

April 27 1986, Imola (Italy)

After two seasons with 220 litres of fuel available, the powerful turbo engines were allowed only 195 litres per Grand Prix in 1986. For the two opening rounds at the relatively slow Jacarepagua (Brazil) and Jerez (Spain) circuits, this was not a big problem, but the reduced fuel limit turned the round three, San Marino Grand Prix at the high-speed Imola circuit, into a farce. In the final laps, Michele Alboreto (Ferrari), Marc Surer (Arrows-BMW – photo), Keke Rosberg (McLaren-TAG) and Ricardo Patrese (Brabham-BMW) all ran out of fuel. The McLaren-TAG of race leader Alain Prost began to misfire on the final lap, but by zig-zagging through the final corners, he managed to get the last drops in the fuel tank into the engine. "We are supposed to be racing drivers, yet we spend all our time watching computer rear-outs to tell us when we can go fast. It makes a complete joke of Formula 1," Prost said after the race.

A LIGHTER SHADE OF PALE

September 21 1986, Estoril (Portugal)

The red and white Marlboro colours on the McLarens of the 1970s and 1980s is one of the most iconic liveries in F1 history. Marlboro sponsored McLaren from 1974 to 1996, but on one occasion a Marlboro McLaren was yellow and white instead of the classic red and white. It happened in the 1986 Portuguese Grand Prix, when Marlboro launched its 'light' cigarette on the international market. The Marlboro Light packets were gold and white, but this did not work on a fast-moving F1 car on TV. But maybe yellow and white would work? For the Portuguese Grand Prix, Keke Rosberg's McLaren was painted yellow and white while teammate Alain Prost's car remained the classic red and white design. The Finn retired at half-distance, but Marlboro's marketing people had seen enough. The yellow and white livery was quietly dropped, and the McLaren cars remained in their classic red and white livery for the next 10 years.

NOW – THAT'S NOT FAIR

October 11 1986, Mexico City (Mexico)

Nigel Mansell (left) and Nelson Piquet (right) spent the 1986 and 1987 seasons as Williams-Honda teammates. But they were not really mates. The chemistry was just not right, and the friction between them was only increased by the fact that they were fighting each other for the World Championship both years.

Before the penultimate race of 1986, the Mexican Grand Prix in Mexico City, Mansell was leading Piquet in the championship with Alain Prost (McLaren-TAG) third. In Mexico, Mansell attended a birthday party for BBC's legendary TV commentator Murray Walker and got away with a nasty case of stomach troubles – locally known as 'Montezuma's Revenge'. During practice, Montezuma forced Mansell into the pits several times for quick visits to the toilet. When Piquet realized what was happening, he removed all the toilet paper from the loos close to the Williams pit...

DEER-DEATH EXPERIENCE

August 15 1987, Osterreichring (Austria)

McLaren driver Stefan Johansson (photo) was on a fast lap during practice for the 1987 Austrian Grand Prix when he came over a crest and found a deer in front of him. The animal was beginning to sit down in the middle of the track, and the Swede didn't even have time to brake. "It hit on the left-hand side, and I can remember the sound to this day – awful. It was a massive impact, and it ripped the whole left-side of the car clean off," he said later. Ayrton Senna (Lotus) was behind the McLaren and the Brazilian was showered by what was left of the deer. The accident was not over for Johansson. He had no steering and no brakes and skated across the grass and hit the armco barrier hard. Johansson broke a couple of ribs in the accident, but he still finished a brave seventh in the race.

A $1.5 MILLION COIN TOSS

Autumn 1987, Esher (Great Britain)

In late 1987 Ayrton Senna (right) and McLaren team principal Ron Dennis (left) needed each other. Senna had been driving for Lotus since 1985 and wanted to move to McLaren. Ron Dennis was looking for a new engine supplier to replace the outdated TAG-Porsche V6s. Honda, a keen supporter of Senna, was the obvious choice. A deal with the Brazilian would ensure McLaren not only the fastest driver but also the strongest engine. Dennis and Senna met in the Brazilian's house in Esher, England to discuss a contract for 1988 and beyond, but could not agree on Senna's fee. Discussions went on for a long time, and in the end, there was $500,000 between what Dennis would offer and what Senna wanted. With neither prepared to budge, they decided to toss a coin. Dennis won. Only later did they realize that what they had been negotiating was a three-year contract, so the coin toss actually cost Senna $1.5 million over the term of the contract.

SO CLOSE TO THE PERFECT SCORE

September 11 1988, Monza (Italy)

McLaren-Honda's total domination of the 1988 season was broken at the Italian Grand Prix, the 12th of 16 rounds. The previous 11 Grands Prix had all been won by McLaren team-mates Ayrton Senna or Alain Prost, but the Frenchman retired in Italy with engine problems. Senna was on his way to yet another McLaren win but, with just two laps to go in Monza, it all went wrong when Senna was lapping Jean-Louis Schlesser (Williams-Judd). Schlesser, making his Grand Prix debut standing in for the unwell Nigel Mansell (who was out with chicken pox), tried to get out of Senna's way at the chicane, but the two cars collided. With both McLarens out, Ferrari took its only win of 1988 with Gerhard Berger leading Michele Alboreto home in a popular 1-2. Two weeks later the 1988 season returned to normal with Prost winning the Portuguese Grand Prix in Estoril. Prost and Senna shared the remaining three wins between them. Only two laps at Monza separated McLaren from the perfect score of 16 wins in 16 races.

WORLD CHAMPION WITH FEWER POINTS THAN RUNNER-UP

October 30 1988, Suzuka (Japan)

Ayrton Senna (McLaren-Honda – right) clinched the 1988 World Championship when he won the Japanese Grand Prix in Suzuka. But when the season ended with the Australian Grand Prix in Adelaide two weeks later, his teammate Alain Prost (left) had actually scored 11 points more than the Brazilian. How come? Only the 11 best results from the 16 races counted for the World Championship. Prost, who finished in point scoring positions in 14 races, had to drop 18 points - Senna only had to drop four points and consequently ended up in front of the Frenchman in the final standings.

June 18 1989, Montreal (Canada)

18 DIFFERENT CARS

The 1989 season saw the most varied field ever with 21 teams entered. The Italian Life team succumbed before the first race and withdrew, but 20 teams lined up for the season's 16 races. Although they did not all take part in the races. The big field made pre-qualifying necessary, and the EuroBrun team did not qualify for a single race, while Zakspeed only made the cut twice. The Canadian Grand Prix in Montreal, which saw a Williams-Renault 1-2 with Thierry Boutsen winning in front of Ricardo Patrese (photo), holds the record for the highest number of different constructors in a race: with 18 different makes of cars: AGS, Arrows, Benetton, Brabham, BMS-Dallara, Coloni, Ferrari, Ligier, Lotus, Larrousse-Lola, Leyton House-March, McLaren, Minardi, Onyx, Osella, Rial, Tyrrell and Williams all started the race - while Zakspeed and EuroBrun did not qualify, as usual.

“WHAT BLACK FLAG? WHAT RADIO MESSAGE?”

September 24 1989, Estoril (Portugal)

Nigel Mansell (Ferrari) had a controversial 1989 Portuguese Grand Prix. It all started on lap 39, when he was leading the race. He came into the pits for new tires. Missing the Ferrari pit by a few metres, he reversed back, had his tyres changed and then re-joined the race, in second place behind Ayrton Senna (McLaren-Honda). The regulations clearly state that it is forbidden to reverse in the pit lane, and the stewards had no choice but to disqualify the Englishman. Mansell failed to stop despite being shown the black flag on three consecutive laps. The Ferrari crew also radioed him about his disqualification and hung out a pit board. But Mansell just continued. On lap 49 he caught Senna and dived inside the Brazilian. The Ferrari and the McLaren collided, and both went into the sand trap and retired (photo). Because he had ignored the black flag, the FIA banned Mansell from the following Grand Prix in Spain. And without the points from Portugal, Senna lost the World Championship to teammate and arch-rival Alain Prost...

90's

POWER HORSE
ENERGY-DRINK
BRIDGESTONE
FERRETTI
DANKA
zepter
1
zepter INTERNATIONAL
POWER HORSE ENERGY-DRINK

99 RACES BETWEEN WINS

May 13 1990, Imola (Italy)

For a long time, it looked like Riccardo Patrese's win for Brabham-BMW in the 1983 South African Grand Prix would be his last in Formula 1.
For the next six years, the Italian raced for Alfa Romeo (1984-1985), Brabham again (1986-1987) and in 1988 he signed for Williams. He took a couple of third places in 1984 and 1987, and then four second places during the 1989 season for Williams-Renault. Finally on May 13 1990 he won the San Marino Grand Prix in Imola (photo). It was 99 races – or six years and 210 days - since his 1983 win in South Africa. It is the longest gap between a driver's wins in the history of the Formula 1 World Championship. Patrese didn't stop there: he also won three Grands Prix in 1991 and 1992.

NO TYRES, NO RACE

August 26 1990, Spa-Francorchamps (Belgium)

Peter Monteverdi was a successful businessman in Switzerland. He was also a motor racing enthusiast, and took part in the non-championship Solitude Formula 1 Grand Prix in Germany in 1961 with his own MBM car, although he retired after just two laps. Soon afterwards, the car suffered some kind of a failure and went off into the trees during an event at Hockenheim in much the same way as the accident in which Jim Clark later met his death. Monteverdi was seriously injured but survived. He quit racing, buried the remains of his F1 car in the foundations of a new car showroom in Binningen, and began building his road cars instead. In 1990 he returned to Formula 1, this time as a team owner. He bought the Onyx team and rebranded it Monteverdi. It was a somewhat strange and modest set-up: The team's motorhome was an old London double decker bus and the F1 car suffered from poor preparation. When driver Gregor Foitek was lucky to escape unhurt from a suspension breakage during practice for the Hungarian Grand Prix, he informed Monteverdi that he had had enough and was quitting the team. Brave Finn J.J. Lehto decided to stay on, but to no avail. Before the next Grand Prix in Belgium, Goodyear, which was owed $400,000, refused to supply more tyres until the debt was paid. Monteverdi withdrew from the World Championship and the team was never seen again.

NOT A GREAT SUCCESS

September 30 1990, Jerez (Spain)

Claudio Langes raced in Formula 3000 from 1985 to 1989 with decent results, finishing second in the Enna-Pergusa round in 1989. For 1990, he signed with the EuroBrun F1 team (photo). With 19 teams on the entry list, six teams had to pre-qualify on Friday morning, and EuroBrun was one of them. In the Judd-powered EuroBrun, this was an uphill struggle for Langes, and he failed to pre-qualify for any of the first 14 rounds. His last chance came in the Spanish Grand Prix in Jerez, but he was only sixth of the seven drivers – more than three seconds slower than the leading AGS of Yannick Dalmas (and more than seven seconds off McLaren driver Ayrton Senna's pole position time the following day). With the Japanese and Australian Grands Prix remaining, EuroBrun decided to withdraw from Formula 1, leaving poor Langes as probably the most unsuccessful driver in the history of the sport. His entire F1 career consisted of 14 failed attempts to even pre-qualify. It is said that Langes was not too worried as he insured himself against failure to qualify and ended the year with a big financial pay-off...

HOW TO WIN THE TITLE

October 21 1990, Suzuka, (Japan)

The 1989 World Championship had been decided by a collision between McLaren teammates Ayrton Senna and Alain Prost in the Japanese Grand Prix in Suzuka. In 1990, Prost (by then in a Ferrari) and Senna arrived in Suzuka head-to-head in the championship again. Senna took pole position and requested that pole be on the racing line, on the inside. This was initially granted but the decision was then overturned by FIA President Jean-Marie Balestre. Senna was furious at what he saw as manipulation. "If tomorrow, Prost beats me off the line, at the first corner I will go for it. And he better not turn in, because he is not going to make it," he warned. The Brazilian was true to his word. Prost took the lead from the grippier second position, but Senna did not brake before the first corner – hitting Prost and taking them both out - clinching the World Championship in the process.

A SUICIDE ATTEMPT DURING PRE-QUALIFYING

March 8 1991,
Phoenix (United States)

Pre-qualifying for the 1991 United States Grand Prix at the street circuit in downtown Phoenix was red-flagged after just a few minutes. A man on crutches had hobbled on to the track and lain down in an attempt to commit suicide. He was narrowly missed by Eric van de Poele, who was making his Formula 1 debut for the new Lambo team (photo). "I couldn't believe it," van de Poele said. "It was my first laps in F1 and everything was supposed to be so professional. Then I come round a corner and there is a man lying in the middle of the track..." The man had been released from the Maricopa Medical Centre a few blocks from the circuit earlier in the day. He was taken back to the hospital and pre-qualifying resumed.

JUST DON'T WAVE

June 2 1991,
Montreal (Canada)

Nigel Mansell had dominated the 1991 Canadian Grand Prix from the start. His Williams-Renault teammate Riccardo Patrese started from pole position, but the Englishman took the lead going into the first corner. From there, he built up a big lead, and he was already celebrating when he started the last lap. With one hand busy waving to the crowd, he was too late in engaging a lower gear when the engine revs dropped. The engine cut out and Nelson Piquet (Benetton-Ford) in second place caught and passed the Williams and went on to an unexpected win. Mansell was finally classified sixth. “It's almost unbelievable,” the English man said.

A DAY IN COURT THAT CHANGED F1 HISTORY

August 11 1991, London (Great Britain)

Two days after setting the fastest lap in the 1991 Hungarian Grand Prix for the new Jordan team, Bertrand Gachot (photo) had to appear in court in London. Earlier that year he had had an argument with an aggressive London cab driver on the city's Park Lane. To protect himself the Belgian grabbed a defence spray which he had previously bought for his girlfriend. He sprayed this at his assailant. What Gachot didn't know was that the spray was illegal in Great Britain. Expecting to escape with a fine, Gachot was astonished to be sentenced to six months in prison. This left the Jordan team without a driver for the Belgian Grand Prix a few days later. Jordan offered Gachot's seat to a young German F1 newcomer by the name of Michael Schumacher. The rest, as they say, is history. Gachot later appealed the sentence and it was reduced to two months.

F1 DRIVER KIDNAPPED!

December 13 1991
Maichingen (Germany)

On Friday December 13 1991 ex-F1 driver Hans Herrmann (photo) was on his way home from a Mercedes Christmas party. As he entered his house in Maichingen outside Stuttgart, he faced three masked men. They had tied up his wife Madeleine and knocked out his dog with a gun, and were demanding DM 1 million. They drove off with Herrmann in the boot of his own car. His wife managed to scrape together DM 300,000. Once they had the money, they told her that Hans was still in the boot of his car in a local car park. Herrmann, who finished third in the 1954 Swiss Grand Prix and was the winner of the Le Mans 24 Hours in 1970, was freed. The kidnappers were never brought to justice.

HOME SUPPORT

July 12 1992,
Silverstone (Great Britain)

Nigel Mansell was always popular with the spectators at the British Grand Prix. And the local hero appreciated the support from his fans – he regularly claimed that the fans at his home Grand Prix were worth a few tenths of a second per lap. And he was probably right: from 1986 to 1992 Mansell took the fastest lap in the British Grand Prix seven years in a row!

TEAM PRINCIPAL ARRESTED AFTER QUALIFYING

August 29 1992, Spa-Francorchamps (Belgium)

The Saturday of the 1992 Belgian Grand Prix in Spa-Francorchamps was a surprisingly bad day for the small Andrea Moda team. As usual Roberto Moreno and Perry McCarthy did not qualify – but that had happened at all the other races that year except Monaco, where Moreno, by some miracle, put the uncompetitive car on the grid (only to retire after 11 laps). The real surprise in Spa-Francorchamps was the arrival of several policemen in the Andrea Moda pits. They arrested team principal and owner Andrea Sassetti (left). Earlier in the weekend, bailiffs had tried to impound some of the team's equipment, but Sassetti handed over some paperwork to get them off his back. The judge in Verviers suspected that these were forged and sent officers to Spa-Francorchamps to arrest Sassetti. He spent the night in jail but was released on bail on Saturday morning. When the Andrea Moda trucks arrived for their home Grand Prix in Monza two weeks later, they were refused entry into the paddock. The FIA's F1 Permanent Bureau – consisting of Bernie Ecclestone, FIA president Max Mosley and Ferrari's Luca di Montezemolo - had decided that the team should be banned for bringing the sport into disrepute. The FIA's F1 Commission agreed, and the Andrea Mode team disappeared from Formula 1.

TEAM OWNER KILLS HIMSELF AFTER NINE-HOUR SIEGE

November 29 1992, Munich (Germany)

On November 29 1992 the co-owner of the Larrousse F1 team Klaus Walz shot himself in a German hotel after a nine-hour gun-battle with the police. Walz - using the alias 'Rainer Walldorf' - was the man behind the Comstock Group, which acquired 65% of the Larrousse team in September 1992 (photo). In late October, French and German police officers tried to arrest Walz in his home in Valbonne near Nice in the south of France. He was wanted in connection with four different murders and also suspected of being involved in trafficking stolen luxury cars. Walz seemed to accept his arrest calmly and before leaving with the officers, he asked if he might collect something important from his desk. This was a hand grenade, which helped him escape with a police officer as his hostage. Walz, an occasional Formula 2 driver in the late 1970s, and the officer went off in the German's BMW estate car. He arranged to meet his nephew and left the police officer handcuffed to the steering wheel at the meeting place. The hand grenade was reportedly thrown into a nearby chicken coop. For more than a month the F1 team co-owner was one of Europe's most wanted men. In the last weekend of November, the German police tracked him down to a hotel near Munich. After a gun battle and after a nine-hour siege, Walz killed himself.

It was not the first time the Larrousse team was in the news for the wrong reasons. The team was founded as Larrousse-Calmels by ex-F1 driver and ex-Renault team principal Gerard Larrousse and French businessman Didier Calmels in 1986 and made its debut in 1987. The team changed its name to Equipe Larrousse in early 1989 when Calmels was jailed for six years for fatally shooting his wife Dominique after a 'domestic argument'.

REIGNING CHAMPIONS ENTER TOO LATE

February 25 1993, Paris (France)

The deadline for teams to enter the 1993 Formula 1 World Championship was midnight on Sunday November 15 1992. When the FIA in Paris had not received an application from Williams-Renault on Monday morning (November 16), the reigning Constructors' World Champion (and the team behind 1992 Drivers' World Champion Nigel Mansell) was excluded from the 1993 season. Williams's entry was received in Paris later on the Monday, but the team (and start numbers 1 and 2) was left off the official entry list, which was published in mid-January. It turned out that Williams had sent its entry to Bernie Ecclestone's FOCA office in London instead of the FIA HQ in Paris. "Perhaps we are guilty of some sloppy office work, but the penalty is out of all proportion to the crime," team principal Frank Williams said. To allow Williams into the 1993 World Championship, unanimous agreement of all the other teams was needed. Two teams refused - because Williams had earlier blocked a number of rule changes discussed by the teams. The problem was only solved after two months of sabre rattling and political warfare. It was February 25 – three weeks before the first grand prix in South Africa - when the FIA World Council allowed Williams-Renault back into the World Championship.

THE GREATEST LAP EVER?

April 11 1993,
Donington (Great Britain)

Ayrton Senna's Ford Cosworth V8-powered McLaren was not really competitive in 1993. At least not compared to the Williams cars of Alain Prost and Damon Hill, which had far more power from their Renault V10 engines. For the third race of the season, the European Grand Prix at Donington Park, Prost and Hill qualified on the front row. Senna was fourth; 1.6 seconds behind Prost's pole time. On race day, rain became a great equaliser, and Senna used his supreme wet-weather skills to win the race. The victory was due largely to what was probably the greatest lap in Formula 1 history: At the start, Senna was edged up on the kerb by Michael Schumacher (Benetton-Ford) and lost a position to Karl Wendlinger (Sauber-Ilmor). Accelerating out of the first corner, Senna took fourth place from Schumacher, and then passed Wendlinger on the outside of the high-speed Craner Curves. He then had his sights on Hill, and he passed the Englishman halfway round the lap. In the next couple of corners, Senna reeled in Prost, and he passed the Williams to take the lead under braking for the penultimate corner, the Melbourne Hairpin (photo). A few seconds later he finished the first lap with a lead of 0.6 seconds! Almost two hours later, he had lapped the entire field bar the second-placed Damon Hill.

BUSY FRIDAY FOR SENNA

April 23 1993,
Imola (Italy)

Ayrton Senna had a busy first practice day for the 1993 San Marino Grand Prix (photo). The Brazilian was leading the World Championship after a great win in the previous Grand Prix at Donington Park, but he still hadn't signed a contract for the season with McLaren. The parties could not agree on a financial deal, and in addition to the money matters, Senna was also unhappy with the team's Ford engines. He had started the first three races of the season on race-by-race deals and only decided to go to Imola, where McLaren's reserve driver Mika Hakkinen was lined up to drive his car, at the last possible moment.

Senna flew from his Brazilian home in Sao Paulo on Thursday and arrived in Rome's international Leonardo di Vinci airport early on Friday morning. He jumped into a taxi, which took him to the national airport at Ciampino. There McLaren's executive jet was waiting for him, and it flew him to Bologna airport, from where a helicopter took him to Imola, and a quick ride through the crowds on a scooter brought him to the paddock with about five minutes to go before the first free practice. Not unsurprisingly, he had a small accident after only a few laps, but the following day he qualified fourth in the under-powered McLaren. He retired from the race, but still led the championship when he left Imola. It took another two months of tough negotiations between Senna and McLaren-boss Ron Dennis and four more race-by-race deals before the Brazilian finally signed a 1993 contract - on the eve of the British Grand Prix in July.

September 12 1993, Monza (Italy)

F1 CAREER OVER AFTER 200 METRES

Marco Apicella had been one of the leading contenders in the International Formula 3000 Championship in the early 1990s but never quite made it to Formula 1. In 1992 he switched to the Japanese Formula 3000/Nippon Championship when he finally got a chance to race in F1. Jordan driver Thierry Boutsen had decided to retire before the Italian Grand Prix, and Apicella managed to find sponsorship to secure the drive in his home race. He qualified 23rd and on Sunday the 28-year-old Italian was ready to make his Formula 1 debut. “It was a great day, but I knew I was only going to do this one race, so there was quite a bit of pressure,” he said. It was a chaotic start, which saw Ayrton Senna's McLaren-Ford ride over the Williams-Renault of Damon Hill.

They could both continue, but further back another shunt saw Apicella's race end after just a few seconds: “I did maybe 200 metres before somebody hit me. The steering broke and I had to stop. Even before the first corner...” It was one of the shortest careers in the history of the FIA Formula 1 World Championship, but there was at least consolation for the Italian. One week later he married long-time girlfriend Barbara and one year later he won the Japanese Formula 3000/Nippon series.

SIXTEEN MONTHS AND ONLY WILLIAMS ON POLE

November 6 1993, Adelaide (Australia)

On July 4 1992, Nigel Mansell was fastest in qualifying for the French Grand Prix in Magny Cours in his Williams-Renault. It was the start of an incredible run of pole positions for the British team: Mansell or his team-mate Ricardo Patrese went on to take pole position in all the remaining eight races of the 1992 season. It was all change for Williams-Renault in 1993, when Alain Prost and Damon Hill replaced Mansell and Patrese. But one thing did not change: the dominant Williams-Renault started from pole position in every race. Only in the last race of 1993, the Australian Grand Prix in Adelaide, did Ayrton Senna (McLaren-Ford) manage to break the Williams-Renault monopoly on pole position, which had lasted for more than 16 months.

PACIFIC DNQ FOR PACIFIC GRAND PRIX

April 17 1994,
Aida (Japan)

The Tanaka International Circuit near Aida in Japan hosted its first Grand Prix in April 1994. With the Japanese Grand Prix firmly established in Suzuka, the race in Aida was given the title 'Pacific Grand Prix.' The small circuit was not very interesting, but it still made history. It was the first and only time a team had the same name as the Grand Prix. The Pacific team with Bertand Gachot and Paul Belmondo had made their F1 debut only three weeks earlier in the opening round of the 1994 season in Brazil, where Belmondo failed to qualify and Gachot retired on the first lap. Things went from bad to worse in their 'home' Grand Prix in Aida, when both Pacific drivers failed to qualify for the Pacific Grand Prix. Pacific – both the team and the Grand Prix – disappeared from Formula 1 after the 1995 season.

ONE SEASON, THREE TEAMS

October 16 1994, Jerez (Spain)

In the 1950s it was not unusual for drivers to change teams during the season. A couple of examples from 1954: The reigning world champion Alberto Ascari was contracted to Lancia, but the new car was not ready until late in the season, and Ascari drove for Maserati in the French and British Grand Prix and for Ferrari in Italy. Juan-Manuel Fangio started the season with Maserati but moved to Mercedes when the German manufacturer entered Formula 1 at midseason (and won the championship). In modern times drivers are locked into long-term commitments to their team, but in 1994 Johnny Herbert drove for three different teams in the course of the season. The Englishman started the year with Lotus, but the team went into administration after the Italian Grand Prix. For the following race, the European Grand Prix in Jerez, Herbert was in a Ligier (photo). At the time, the French team was owned by Benetton team principal Flavio Briatore, and with Benetton in a close fight with Williams for the Constructors' Championship, Herbert's Ligier career was just a one-off affair: In the last two races of the season, the young Englishman partnered Michael Schumacher in the Benetton team. While the German took the Drivers' title, Herbert retired from both races and Williams won the Constructors' championship.

MISSED FOUR RACES AND HE STILL WON THE TITLE

November 13 1994, Adelaide (Australia)

When Michael Schumacher (Benetton-Ford) crashed into Damon Hill (Williams-Renault) in the final round of the 1994 World Championship in Adelaide (photo), he clinched the title. Quite a feat – considering the German had missed four of the year's 16 Grands Prix. He was disqualified from second place in the British Grand Prix for ignoring the black flag and was also given a two-race ban, which saw him miss the Italian and Portuguese Grands Prix. Schumacher was also disqualified from the Belgian Grand Prix, where he finished first, because of excessive wear on the wooden skid block under the car.

YES, GOVERNOR – YOU'RE STILL QUICK

April 6 1995,
Buenos Aires (Argentina)

Carlos Reutemann was 52 years old and the governor of the Santa Fe province when he visited the 1995 Argentina Grand Prix at the Autodromo in Buenos Aires. He had not driven a Formula 1 car in 13 years. Ferrari, the team he drove for in 1977-1978, invited him to try one of its 1994 cars on the Thursday, and he immediately impressed onlookers: Reutemann's best lap time – on a wet track – would have placed him 11th. in the session for the regular drivers held a few hours earlier!

MANSELL AND THE $500,000 BIG-MAC

May 14 1995,
Circuit de Catalunya (Spain)

The 1995 Spanish Grand Prix was only Nigel Mansell's second race for McLaren (photo), but it was also his last. He retired from the race at the Circuit de Catalunya on lap 18 due to...well, it was reported that he just 'gave up'. It was the culmination of a difficult time for the 1992 World Champion, who was never seen racing in F1 again. A few days after the race in Spain, McLaren announced that "Following extensive and open discussion, Marlboro McLaren Mercedes and Nigel Mansell have decided to end their current Formula 1 agreement".

It had started only a few months earlier. After winning the 1992 title, Mansell spent two years in the American CART series, but made a comeback to F1, when he took Ayrton Senna's Williams seat after the Brazilian's fatal accident in a handful of 1994 races. Williams, which had already broken up with Mansell in controversial circumstances back in 1992, did not want to continue the new relationship into 1995, and in February the Englishman signed with McLaren. Maybe the McLaren designers were over-ambitious with the team's new car; maybe two years in the States had made Mansell slightly bigger than before, in any case, during the first tests of the MP4/10, both Mansell and teammate Mika Hakkinen suffered a serious lack of cockpit space. The

Finn's problems were solved with modifications, but there was just not enough room for the bigger Englishman. A few days before the first race of the season, it was announced that Mansell would be replaced by his countryman Mark Blundell in both Brazil and Argentina while McLaren started work on a XL-version of the MP4/10. The cost, according to McLaren boss Ron Dennis was "half a million dollars". The 'Big Mac' was ready for the San Marino Grand Prix, where Mansell qualified ninth and finished 10th but he was clearly still not comfortable with the car. Then came Spain and the sad end to a great F1 career.

MAY 27 1995,
Monte Carlo (Monaco)

INOUE ROLLS AFTER CRASH WITH SAFETY CAR

Taki Inoue's difficult debut season in Formula 1 went from bad to worse immediately after Saturday morning's free practice for the 1995 Monaco Grand Prix. The Japanese Footwork-Arrows driver was being towed back to the pits behind a truck when the Renault Maxi Clio Safety Car (driven by ex-rally driver Jean Ragnotti with FIA Press Delegate Francesco Longanesi in the passenger seat) arrived at high speed. The Renault hit the Footwork-Arrows with such force that the F1 car overturned. "I just heard a screech of brakes and then felt a massive impact," Inoue said. The Japanese, wearing his crash helmet but not the seat belts, was lucky to escape with only light injuries. He was hauled out in a semi-conscious state (photo) and was not permitted to take part in final qualifying a few hours after the crash. "It was an enormous whack," an angry Footwork-Arrows team principal Jackie Oliver said. "Everything is destroyed - gearbox, casing, engine - everything."

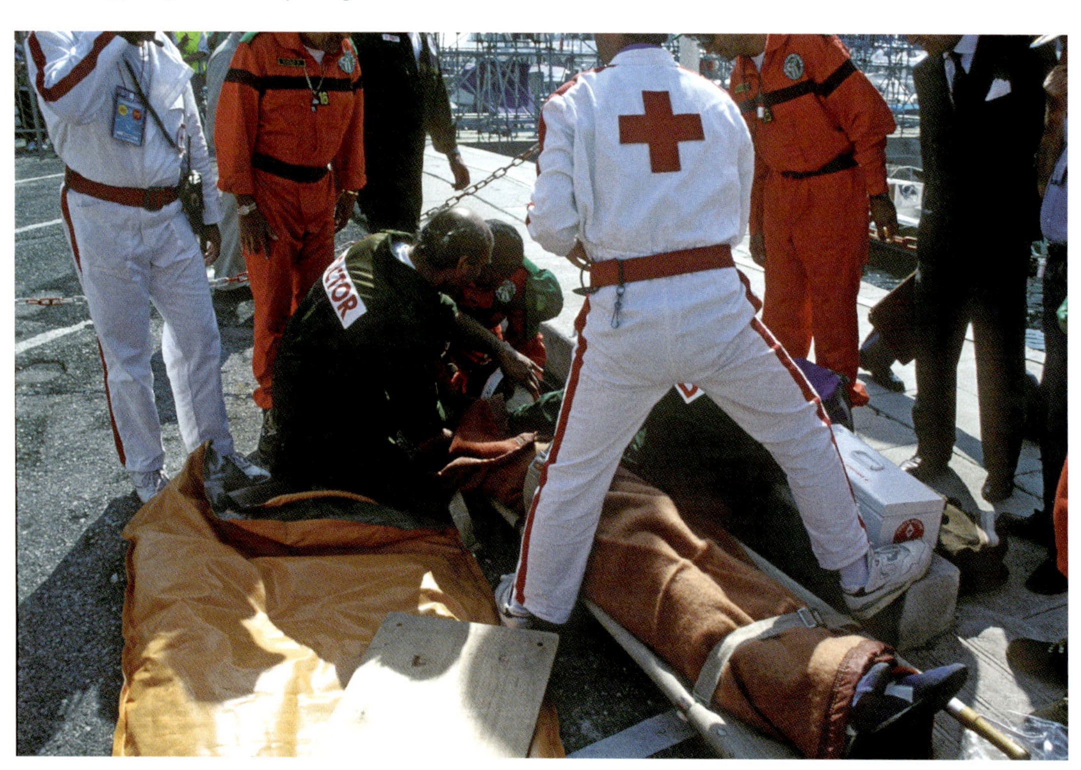

PIT? MOI?

March 9 1997, Albert Park (Australia)

Jean Alesi (Benetton-Renault) had a busy Australian Grand Prix in 1997 (photo) – at least until lap 35. He was following Mika Hakkinen (McLaren-Mercedes) and was up to third place at half-distance. The Frenchman was scheduled to pit on lap 31, but urgent radio messages and frantically waved pit boards failed to get his attention - for four laps.

Not surprisingly, the Benetton ran out of fuel. Team boss Flavio Briatore was not impressed, and technical director Nick Wirth refused to comment: “You'd better ask Jean,” was his response to questions from reporters on why the car had stopped. Alesi himself did not hang around to speak to the press.

A LAP WITHOUT THE DRIVER ABOARD

May 25 1997,
Circuit de Catalunya (Spain)

Damon Hill's Arrows-Yamaha (photo) stopped with engine problems just before the finish line at the end of lap 17 of the 1997 Spanish Grand Prix. But the official result credits him with 18 laps – with the final lap taking over 30 minutes. This happened because marshals and team members pushed the car into the pits, and took it across the finish line while the race was still going and so to register the completion of his 18th lap.

Technically, the Arrows-Yamaha completed the final lap without the driver aboard!

WHEN FATE AND JUSTICE DECIDED THE CHAMPIONSHIP

October 26 1997, Jerez (Spain)

The final race of the 1997 season, the European Grand Prix in Jerez, was a classic shoot-out for the World Championship between Michael Schumacher (Ferrari) and Jacques Villeneuve (Williams-Renault). Before the race, the German had a one-point lead, but qualifying proved just how closely matched they were. They set identical lap times, but Schumacher was granted pole position as he had set his time first. Incredibly, Villeneuve's team-mate Heinz-Harald Frentzen then also set exactly the same lap time and started from third position. At the start, Schumacher took the lead but came under pressure from Villeneuve towards the end. Twenty-two laps before the chequered flag, Villeneuve attacked the Ferrari under braking and the two cars were side by side when Schumacher turned into the Williams. If both drivers had retired, Schumacher would take the title, but fate intervened.

The Ferrari was too damaged to continue, but Villeneuve's Williams went on and the Canadian finished third and won the World Championship. Two weeks later, Schumacher was excluded from the entire 1997 season for his unsporting manoeuvre against Villeneuve in Jerez.

FERRARI ATTACKS MCLAREN-WILLIAMS PACT

October 26 1997, Jerez (Spain)

Ferrari was not happy to lose the 1997 World Championship after Michael Schumacher's controversial crash with Jacques Villeneuve (Williams-Renault) in the final round in Jerez. During the race, the Scuderia somehow gained access to the radio communication between the Williams drivers and the team. Ferrari claimed that McLaren and Williams had reached an agreement before the race, in which McLaren drivers Mika Hakkinen (right) and David Coulthard (left) would support Villeneuve's (centre) title bid in return for being given an easy passage to race victory. Hakkinen won the race in front of Coulthard, and towards the end of the race, it looked like the two McLaren drivers acted as a buffer between Villeneuve and Schumacher's Ferrari team-mate Eddie Irvine. Ferrari felt their recordings proved that McLaren and Williams had 'fixed' the race and presented tapes and transcripts to both the British newspaper The Times and FIA. McLaren and Williams both denied that there had been any collusion, and they were cleared by the FIA after a hearing in November 1997. Quite how Ferrari had gained access to their rivals radio communication was never explained.

July 12 1998, Silverstone (Great Britain)

A few minutes before the start of the 1998 British Grand Prix at Silverstone, a spectator decided to join the fun on the track. To stand out from the usual VIPs on the grid, he was stark naked. Exactly how he scaled the safety fences – complete with barbed wire on top - and what he might have left behind on the way, is one of the more delicate mysteries of modern F1 history. The streaker was quickly arrested and taken away by the police. This time through the gates.

THE NAKED TRUTH

TESTING, JUST TESTING

Most weeks, 1999-09, Fiorano or Mugello (Italy

When Luca Badoer won the 1992 Formula 3000 title, he looked to be on his way to a great F1 career. He signed with BMS Scuderia Italia for 1993, but seventh place in the San Marino Grand Prix was his best result. Further seasons with Minardi (1995 and 1999) and Forti (1996) did not improve his results, and from 2000 he focussed on a new job as Ferrari's test driver.

The Prancing Horse certainly kept him busy: with no restrictions on testing and two private tracks in Fiorano and Mugello, Ferrari tested a LOT. Badoer stayed with Ferrari for 10 years until the end of 2010, and according to unofficial statistics, he covered a total of 131,944 kms in testing. That is more than 400 Grand Prix distances – or almost four times around the world. After 10 years of loyal testing, Badoer was finally given a chance to race for Ferrari in a Grand Prix when Felipe Massa was injured in 2009. It was not a success, and he quietly returned to testing after only two races.

SPLIT PERSONALITY

January 6 1999, Brackley (Great Britain)

The new British American Racing (BAR) team announced its 1999 plans at the factory in Brackley in early January with two BAR 01s on display. Team owner British American Tobacco wanted to maximise its F1 involvement by advertising two of its cigarette brands and planned to race one car in 555 livery and one in Lucky Strike colours. This was against the F1 rules, which stated that a team had to run their cars in 'substantially the same livery'. BAR Managing Director Craig Pollock did not see why he couldn't decorate his cars in whatever colours he chose and launched legal actions against the FIA. "We have already clearly demonstrated that we will do everything possible to be a serious contender in Formula 1 and therefore have no choice but to take all steps available to protect our interests," he said. BAR lost the fight and had to come up with a compromise livery incorporating both brands.

A MONTH IN POLITICS

November 11 1999, London (Great Britain)

In 1999 the EU was working on a ban on tobacco advertising. At the time, all the leading F1 teams were sponsored by tobacco brands (Rothmans-Williams, West-McLaren, Marlboro-Ferrari, Mild Seven-Benetton, Benson & Hedges-Jordan, Gauloises-Prost) and it was clear a ban would have a big impact on the sport. The British Labour government supported the ban, and on October 16, FIA president Max Mosley and Bernie Ecclestone (photo) met Prime Minister Tony Blair to discuss the matter in 10 Downing Street. Two weeks later the Health Minister Tessa Jowell announced a Labour U-turn on tobacco sponsorship – it wanted F1 to be exempt from the proposed EU ban. The following day it was revealed that Jowell's husband David Mills had been a director of the Mild Seven Benetton team and was the team's legal advisor. On November 11 Labour admitted that Ecclestone had donated £1 million to the party in 1997 – and it was revealed that another donation was discussed during the meeting in October. Prime Minister Tony Blair decided to return the money to Ecclestone – who initially refused to accept it. The end result was that cigarette brands were prominent F1 sponsors for another seven years. And 'A Bernie' became slang in the City of London for £1 million...

CRASH TEST DUMMY

December 11 1999,
Circuit de Catalunya (Spain)

Pedro Diniz was in his fifth Formula 1 season in 1999. But his crash record shows experience isn't everything. He crashed out of 10 of the season's 16 Grands Prix – the remaining accidents came during testing, practice and qualifying. When he finished the season with a test at the Circuit de Catalunya outside Barcelona, the Brazilian crashed his Sauber-Petronas for the 30th time!

HSBC
noble group
noble group
noble group
noble group
noble group
noble group
150
100
50

CARS NUMBER 1 TO 7 – TAKE YOUR GRID POSITIONS

March 12 2000,
Albert Park (Australia)

The first seven positions on the grid for the 2000 Australian Grand Prix in Melbourne's Albert Park were taken by cars numbered 1 – 7. The reigning Constructors' World Champions McLaren-Mercedes had the first two places on the grid with World Champion Mika Hakkinen (1) and David Coulthard (2). The second row consisted of Ferrari drivers Michael Schumer (3 – photo)) and Rubens Barrichello (4) with Jordan-Mugen's Heinz-Harald Frentzen (5) and Jarno Trulli (6) on row three. Eddie Irvine in his Jaguar with starting number 7 was seventh, but then Jacques Villeneuve in his BAR-Honda (car number 22) ruined the symmetry in eighth place. The race was won by Michael Schumacher in front of Rubens Barrichello and Ralf Schumacher (in his Williams-BMW #9).

RED BULL WITH BROKEN WINGS

March 25 2000,
Interlagos, (Brazil)

After qualifying for the 2000 Brazilian Grand Prix in Interlagos, the Red Bull sponsored Sauber-Petronas team decided to withdraw both its cars driven by Mika Salo and Pedro Diniz (photo).

The Finn had a big accident when his rear wing detached itself in Saturday's free practice, and the Brazilian was lucky to escape when his car suffered a similar failure in qualifying. "Here at the track it is not possible for us to analyze the cause of the problem to our satisfaction so we have no option but to withdraw from the race," team boss Peter Sauber explained. A full investigation back at the factory in Hinwil concluded that it was the infamous bumpy Interlagos circuit that caused the failures. "The very severe bumps resulted in both cars undergoing impact loads that were in excess of the cycle predicted during the design of the cars, which in itself incorporated a safety margin," the team explained.

UNDERWEIGHT TO OVER-ACHIEVE

February 14 2001, Estoril (Portugal)

Prost-Peugeot finished last in the 2000 Constructors World Championship, but pre-season testing in 2001 suggested that things would improve dramatically for the cash-strapped team. Jean Alesi was second-fastest at the Circuit de Catalunya in the new Ferrari-powered Prost's first test. The real shock came on February 14 when Alesi was more than a second faster round Estoril than anybody else. The impressive test times suddenly made 2000's backmarker a promising proposition for sponsors, and several deals were signed before the first 2001 race in Australia. But in Melbourne Alesi qualified 14th and team-mate Gaston Mazzacane (photo) was 20th. It turned out the car had been massively under-weight during testing, and only when the sponsors had been secured, did the car show its true form.

The team scored only four points during the year and went bankrupt in early 2002 – exactly a year after the 'sensational' lap times from the Estoril test.

RAIKKONEN ON PROBATION FOR F1 DEBUT

March 4 2001, Albert Park (Australia)

The 21-year old Finn Kimi Raikkonen was effectively 'on probation' when he made his F1 debut with Sauber at the start of 2001. The rookie had only done 23 car races in his career when he signed for the Swiss team and came straight from the British Formula Renault Championship. The FIA was hesitant to issue the inexperienced Finn with a Superlicence, but after some impressive testing in late 2000 and early 2001, it was agreed Raikkonen would get the first four races of the season to prove he deserved a place in F1. "I understand the FIA's arguments and I have accepted them," Sauber team principal Peter Sauber said. "However, we believe Kimi is up to it." Raikkonen proved just that by taking a strong sixth place in his first Grand Prix in Melbourne (photo), and a permanent Superlicence was duly issued.

A STEERING WHEEL COMES LOOSE

April 15 2001, Imola (Italy)

Kimi Raikkonen's 2001 San Marino Grand Prix came to an unusual end when his steering wheel came loose on the 18th lap. Not unsurprisingly, he lost control of the Sauber-Petronas and crashed into the barrier. "I don't know why it happened – as far as I am concerned, I put it on correctly." The Sauber team launched a full investigation of the incident, and it was discovered that the steering wheel could be yanked off if it was twisted and pulled very strongly at the same time. Modifications were made before the next Grand Prix in Spain.

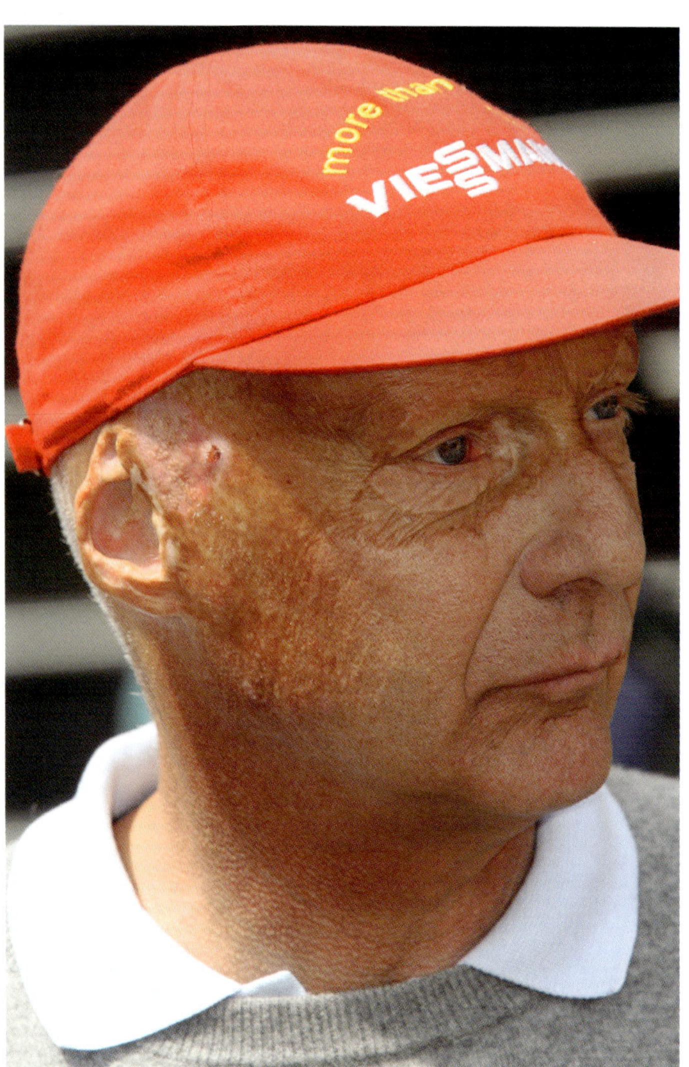

EAR LOST AND FOUND

June 21 2001, Nürburgring (Germany)

Niki Lauda returned to the Nürburgring 25 years after he nearly lost his life – and most of his right ear - in an accident during the 1976 German Grand Prix.

The Austrian was there for the European Grand Prix weekend and the RTL TV station wanted to mark the anniversary with an interview at Bergwerk, the scene of the crash. Before the accident, Lauda and a friend, restaurateur and star-caterer Karl-Heinz Zimmermann, decided to lighten the mood, and Zimmermann bought a pig ear at a local butcher. When the interview started, Lauda talked about how he lost control of the Ferrari, where the car had hit the armco, how it caught fire and how he was pulled out of the flames by fellow-driver Arturo Merzario. Then he bent down in the grass and said: “Bloody Hell – look what I found” and picked up the pig ear. Needless to say – the TV crew and later the viewers were somewhat surprised.

BLACK NOSE FOR FERRARI

September 16 2001, Monza (Italy):

The 2001 Italian Grand Prix came just five days after the 9/11 terrorist attacks in New York and Washington DC. The FIA announced that the race would go ahead as scheduled, and several teams put American flags on their cars as a mark of respect for the victims. In agreement with their partners, Ferrari decided to take all sponsor logos off their cars and ran with black nosecones on the cars of Michael Schumacher and Rubens Barrichello.

COME ON, BOYS - LIFT HER UP

March 2 2002, Albert Park, Australia

Mark Webber was very much the hometown hero when he made his Formula 1 debut in the 2002 Australian Grand Prix (photo). But his Minardi was not competitive, and he qualified in only 18th place. Minardi had not scored points for almost three years, but a few strong marshals in the first corner changed that. A crash at the start left seven cars out of the race and Webber in an unexpected eighth place. The race was about to be red-flagged, which would have meant Webber would return to the back of the field. The Aussie marshals sensed that this was Webber's big chance - but only if the race continued. With cranes and trucks, six of the seven cars in the first corner were quickly removed but there was no crane for the last one, a Sauber.

So eight strong marshals took things in their own hands and physically lifted the Sauber and carried it off the track - just in time for the race to continue. Webber seized the opportunity and finished his first Grand Prix in a sensational fifth place.

A SAUBER HITS THE MEDICAL CAR

March 31 2002,
Interlagos (Brazil)

Sauber-driver Nick Heidfeld was lucky to escape injury after he hit the medical car carrying Professor Sid Watkins during the Sunday morning warm-up to the 2002 Brazilian Grand Prix in Interlagos. The German did not see the red flags brought out after Enrique Bernoldi crashed his Arrows and blocked the track in the first corner. Heidfeld arrived at high speed and narrowly missed the Arrows but then smashed into the door of the medical car, which had just been opened by its driver, ex-F1 driver Alex Ribeiro. "I didn't see the flags as my view was blocked by a Ferrari ahead of me. When I saw Bernoldi's car, I had nowhere to go, but I saw a space on the left. Then the door of the medical car opened in front of me and I couldn't avoid hitting it," Heidfeld explained. His Sauber was repaired for the race and Ribeiro and Professor Watkins switched to the spare medical car.

WORLD CHAMPION IN JULY

July 21 2002,
Magny Cours (France)

The 2002 Formula 1 World Championship consisted of 17 races but the fight for the title was already decided by July. Michael Schumacher (Ferrari) had been in a class of his own in the early part of the season, winning seven of the first 10 races. When he took victory in the French Grand Prix in Magny Cours on July 21, it was all over, the German had clinched the World Championship with six races still to go.

SCHUMACHER'S MISTAKE HANDS WIN TO BARRICHELLO

September 29 2002, Indianapolis (United States)

After a season dominated by Ferrari, Michael Schumacher wanted to stage a photo finish at Indianapolis, the penultimate race of the 2002 season.

Having led the race from the start, the German slowed in the last corner to allow his Ferrari team-mate Rubens Barrichello to pull alongside before the finish line, but Michael slowed a bit more than necessary, Barrichello got ahead, but as the Brazilian slowed to let Schumacher back into first place, it was too late. The finish line was not at the famous line of bricks where the chequered flag was waved – the official timing beam was some 20 metres earlier, when Barrichello (right(was 0.011 second in front of the German (left).

Schumacher still thought he had won and waved enthusiastically to the crowd on the first part of the slowing down lap, which he completed in front of his team-mate. When the Ferrari team informed him on the radio that Barrichello was the official winner, the waving stopped. At the press conference after the race, Schumacher – who had clinched the World Championship several weeks earlier – seemed more than a little confused by his second place. "Tell me – where is the finish line actually?" he asked the journalists.

DISHWASHER SPINS

April 6 2003, Interlagos (Brazil)

The 2003 Brazilian Grand Prix was a very wet affair with several storm fronts making their way across the circuit during the afternoon. But even when the rain eased off and the rest of the track was relatively dry, the third corner, the Curva do Sol, remained wet and slippery. Several drivers spun off there – including reigning World Champion Michael Schumacher (Ferrari – photo) and Juan-Pablo Montoya (Williams-BMW). Thirteen years later the real reason for the slippery Curva do Sol was revealed: a drain pipe from the Paddock Club was pouring soapy water on to the Curva de Sol making it as slippery as ice.

A LATE WIN

April 18 2003,
Imola (Italy)

When Fernando Alonso (Renault) crashed heavily, the 2003 Brazilian Grand Prix was red-flagged after what was initially thought to be 55 laps. Kimi Raikkonen (McLaren-Mercedes) was declared the winner, and the Finn received the winner's trophy on the podium watched by a heart-broken Giancarlo Fisichella (Jordan-Ford). The Italian, still chasing his first Grand Prix win after 110 race starts, had passed Raikkonen on lap 54, but the rules stated that in the event of a stoppage, the results should be taken from two laps before. When the Jordan team had a closer look at their lap chart, it turned out that Fisichella had actually started his 56th. lap before the red flag came out. Team principal Eddie Jordan asked the FIA for an investigation, and a few days later, Fisichella was declared the race winner. The FIA ruled that the result should have been taken after 54 laps. At the next race, the San Marino Grand Prix in Fisichella's native Italy, Raikkonen sportingly handed over the trophy in an impromptu ceremony before practice (photo).

NO OVERTAKING

June 1 2003, Monte Carlo (Monaco)

Overtaking is notoriously difficult in Monte Carlo – that's a fact. But a race with absolutely no overtakes? That was what happened in the 2003 Monaco Grand Prix. It was the first of only two races with no overtakes in the history of the FIA Formula 1 World Championship (the other being the 2009 European Grand Prix in Valencia), but it was still an interesting afternoon. And the lead actually changed a few times, but only when the leaders pitted. Ralf Schumacher (Williams-BMW) took the lead from pole (photo), and his team-mate Juan-Pablo Montoya, Kimi Raikkonen (McLaren-Mercedes), Jarno Trulli (Renault) and Michael Schumacher (Ferrari) also took turns in the lead. At the chequered flag, race winner Montoya and Raikkonen and Schumacher in second and third place were covered by less than two seconds. The 2003 Monaco Grand Prix was one of the better races in the principality – even with no overtaking whatsoever.

SPONSORSHIP GONE WRONG

October 12 2003,
Suzuka, Japan

Formula 1 history is filled with sponsors who didn't pay the teams as expected. The usual reaction from the team is to remove the sponsor's name from the car and take them to court. In 2003 the owner of the Minardi team Paul Stoddard adopted a different approach when the company Stayer defaulted on the agreed payments. When another cheque bounced, he kept the name on the car - but with a 'Not Paid' sticker on top of it...

LAUNCH IN MAFIA COUNTRY

January 29 2004, Palermo (Sicily)

Renault team boss Flavio Briatore knew how to throw a party and the 2004 team launch was no exception. More than 600 media and VIP guests attended the unveiling of the Renault RS24 in the largest opera house in Italy, the Teatro Massimo in Palermo, Sicily (photo). After the official launch, Fernando Alonso took the new car out for a demonstration run on the streets of Palermo, but his donuts went wrong, and he stalled. The crowd then broke the barriers to get close to the car and the driver, and Alonso had to make a quick escape and abandon the car. When the Renault mechanics finally managed to recover the team's new car, several bits, including the steering wheel, were missing.

DIAMONDS ARE (NOT) FOREVER

May 23 2004,
Monte Carlo (Monaco)

It was a brilliant PR coup, but it went badly wrong. Jaguar Racing celebrated a new sponsorship deal with diamond company Steinmetz by incorporating a diamond worth $200,000 into the nose of Christian Klien's car in the Monaco Grand Prix. The idea created a buzz in the media – but the column inches proved expensive when Klien crashes nose first into the barriers at the Loews hairpin on the opening lap.

"His car returned to the garage minus the flawless diamond," the Jaguar press release reported drily after the race. "We may not have got the best result on the track, but we have certainly left our mark in Monaco by adding to the glamour. Somebody is going to walk away with more than just as normal motor racing keepsake," team spokesman Nav Sidhu added.

QUALIFYING HIT BY TYPHOON MA-ON

October 10 2004, Suzuka (Japan)

Qualifying for the 2004 Japanese Grand Prix had to be postponed as Typhoon Ma-On was approaching Suzuka. Only 10 days after Typhoon Mari had killed 24 people further up the coast, the organisers decided to close the Suzuka circuit on Saturday and qualifying was rescheduled to Sunday morning. The prospect of a full day without competition was too much for many of the drivers, and Michael Schumacher, Rubens Barrichello, Felipe Massa and others staged an impromptu tournament at the Circuit Hotel's bowling alley. Happily, forecasts that Ma-On was moving directly for Suzuka proved wrong, and it headed instead for Nagoya and Tokyo, although both cities escaped lightly. Qualifying and the race went ahead under sunny skies.

LOTS OF PRACTICE BUT NO RACING

October 22 2004, Interlagos, Brazil

On Friday October 22 2004 Björn Wirdheim had his 19th free practice day in Formula 1. The Swede, who won the 2003 Formula 3000 title, was Jordan's third driver in practice for the 2003 United States Grand Prix and had the same role for Jaguar at all 18 2004 Grands Prix (photo). Wirdheim never progressed to a race seat, and 19 free practice days and no race start is one of the more unusual Formula 1 records. Neel Jani was Toro Rosso's 'Friday driver' at all 18 Grands Prix in 2006 and never took part in a F1 race. Wirdheim later became a TV pundit for Swedish TV while Jani became simulator driver for the new Audi F1 team.

ONLY SIX CARS ON THE GRID

June 19 2005, Indianapolis (United States)

The 2005 tyre war between Bridgestone and Michelin reduced the United States Grand Prix in Indianapolis to a farce. During practice, it became clear that Michelin's tyres were not safe for the high cornering forces generated in the banked corner leading up to the start/finish line. Ralf Schumacher (Toyota) crashed heavily during practice due to tyre failure, and it was obvious that the Michelin tyres would be too dangerous for a race distance. It was impossible to air freight new tyres in at short notice and plans to introduce a chicane before the banked corner were vetoed by the FIA. The 'tyre-gate' affair turned into a power struggle between the teams, the tyre manufacturers, Bernie Ecclestone, FIA president Max Mosley and the promoters in Indianapolis. In the end, the whole field went onto the grid, but the Michelin runners – 14 of the 20 cars entered for the race – retired at the end of the parade lap (photo). Only the Bridgestone runners: Ferrari, Midland-Jordan and Minardi started the race with Ferrari drivers Michael Schumacher and Rubens Barrichello in a class of their own. The US fans were not impressed and booed the teams and drivers. Ten days later, Michelin agreed to refund the spectators' tickets.

NAKED JOURNALIST LAPS SILVERSTONE

July 10 2005, Silverstone (Great Britain)

McLaren-Mercedes had a bad start to the 2004 season, and F1 journalist Bob McKenzie wrote in Daily Express, that he "would run around Silverstone naked" if the team won a race during the season. When Kimi Raikkonen won the Belgian Grand Prix in Spa-Francorchamps, McLaren team principal Ron Dennis (left) was quick to remind the Scotsman about his promise. McKenzie did the honourable thing, went into training – and an hour before the 2005 British Grand Prix, he was ready at the Silverstone start-finish straight. As always, Dennis was kind to the media: "It would be unfair to insist Bob runs completely naked," he said. "He can wear trainers..." His body painted in McLaren colours, McKenzie completed his lap in front of the 100,000 spectators, wearing a strategically-placed puch called a sporran – a traditional part of Highland dress which hangs in front of a kilt and serves as a pocket...

HOW FAST CAN YOU GO?

November 5 2005, Mojave Airport (United States)

What is the top speed of a modern Formula 1 car? It is a difficult question to answer, because even at the high-speed Monza circuit, there is always a corner coming up to slow you down. But in 2005 the BAR-Honda team decided to find out, and built a special high-speed F1 car, which they planned to take to the Bonneville Salt Flat to establish an official speed record for F1 cars. The car, which had test driver Alan van der Merwe behind the wheel, was fitted with a 'rudder', which would help bring the car back under control if it became unstable at the high speeds. The rudder, which was hydraulically controlled and linked to the car's main computer, was the only thing not strictly in adherence with F1 regulations, which outlaws 'moveable aerodynamic devices'.

After a few test runs on the salt flats, the high-speed BAR was ready, but by then the salt flats were flooded. Instead, the team headed to the Mojave Air and Space Port (spacecrafts are launched from here!) and its 3.8 km long runway. The asphalt offered better grip than the salt flats, and the rudder was disabled, making the car fully compliant to the 2005 F1 regulations. The top speed was 413.205 km/h.

JUVENILE DELINQUENT

August 26 2006, Istanbul Park (Turkey)

At the 2006 Turkish Grand Prix, Sebastian Vettel became the youngest driver up to that point to take part in a Grand Prix meeting – the young German was only 19 years and 53 days when he drove a third BMW in the two Friday practice sessions. He also established another record – he was only nine seconds into his F1 career when he broke the rules: He was fined for pit lane speeding on his way out to his first practice laps (photo)! Later on Friday Vettel proved he was also quick on the actual circuit, when he set the fastest lap in the afternoon session.

Two weeks later Vettel also took part in the Friday sessions before the Italian Grand Prix, this time topping both sessions.

F1 V F16

April 20 2007, Volkel (Holland)

Who is fastest – a Formula 1 driver or a jet pilot? Spyker-Ferrari driver Christijan Albers and Royal Dutch Air Force pilot Ralph Aarts provided the answer in 2007. A 1 km race between a Spyker-Ferrari F8-VII and a F16 plane was staged at the Volkel air base in the south of Holland. The two machines lined up side-by-side on separate runways, and at the green light, the F1 was fastest. Albers had a solid advantage after 300 metres, but then everything changed. Over the final 700 metres, the F16 pulled ahead to win the tight race by only two car lengths. Reaching a speed of 450 km/h at the finish line, the fighter plane completed the 1 km race in just 15.5 seconds. "It was pretty close, but in the end, I was very pleased to out-run a F1 car," Aarts said. "It was not a surprise that the Spyker out-accelerated me at the start – but I was also sure that if we ran for long enough, I would get back in front. The key was to find a distance, which suited both of us, and 1 kilometre was probably fair. After the first 300 metres I began to catch Christijan, and just before the finish line – and just before I took off – I passed him," the Royal Dutch Air Force pilot went on. F1 driver Christijan Albers was not too disappointed to finish second to a F16. "It was close, and for the first 300 metres all I could see was the plane in my mirrors," he said." Then he just accelerated past me and off into the distance."

WITH A LITTLE HELP FROM A CRANE

July 22 2007, Nürburgring (Germany)

It was dry when the parade lap for the 2007 European Grand Prix started, but black clouds were hanging over the Nürburgring. A drizzle began when the cars lined up on the grid, and almost immediately after the red lights went off, it began to rain heavily. At the start of the third lap, several cars went off in the first corner including World Championship leader Lewis Hamilton (McLaren-Mercedes). But while Jenson Button, Nico Rosberg, Adrian Sutil, Scott Speed and Vitantonio Liuzzi all retired on the spot, Hamilton stayed in his car and kept the engine running. A crane arrived and lifted the McLar-en out of the gravel and back onto the track. Hamilton was able to continue in the race, and he finished in ninth place, just missing out on a championship point (awarded to the top eight finishers in those days).

STARTED FROM BOTH ENDS OF THE GRID

July 22 2007, Nürburgring (Germany)

At the 2007 European Grand Prix at the Nürburgring it was no surprise that newcomer Markus Winkelhock started his first F1 race from the back row of the grid. His Spyker-Ferrari was not very competitive, and he qualified last. Light rain began when the field lined up on the grid for the start, and Winkelhock decided to begin the race from the pit-lane - on wet-weather tyres. Almost immediately after the start, a huge downpour hit the Nürburgring, and while the rest of the field pitted for new tyres, Winkelhock moved into the lead (photo). The race was red-flagged, and when it was restarted, it was with Winkelhock in pole position. He was soon passed by faster cars, and his first and only Grand Prix ended when he retired after 13 laps with electrical problems. Still – he is one of very few drivers who have led their first Grand Prix. And he is the only driver who has started the same Grand Prix from both ends of the grid.

CARNAGE IN THE PIT-LANE

June 8 2008, Montreal (Canada)

When the Safety Car was deployed in the 2008 Canadian Grand Prix in Montreal, the leaders all went into the pits. There was a red light at the exit, and Kimi Raikkonen (Ferrari) duly stopped. Lewis Hamilton (McLaren-Mercedes) failed to see the red light in time and slammed into the Ferrari. A few moments later, Nico Rosberg (Williams-Toyota) was also inattentive, and clobbered the McLaren. "I don't know what happened," Hamilton said. "I saw the red lights, but by that time, it was too late. I apologise to Kimi for ruining his race, but these things happen." The stewards did not quite see things the same way, and Hamilton (and Rosberg) were given 10-place grid penalties for the next race in France. Kimi Raikkonen? The Iceman just wagged his finger – first at the red light and then at Hamilton.

CRASH TO WIN

September 28 2008, Marina Bay (Singapore)

When Fernando Alonso (Renault) made his first pit-stop in the 2008 Singapore Grand Prix as early as lap 12, it was clear he had a somewhat unusual strategy. But 'unusual' became 'brilliant' just two laps later, when his Renault team-mate Nelson Piquet Jr crashed into the wall. While the rest of the field pitted under the Safety Car, Alonso was promoted to the race lead, and he went on to win the Grand Prix (photo). A year later, when Renault had dropped him, Piquet Jr revealed that he had been told by his team to crash deliberately - to help Alonso. After an investigation by the FIA, the Renault F1 team was charged with conspiracy, and team principal Flavio Briatore and Executive Director of Engineering Pat Symonds left the team. Both eventually received five-year bans from the sport:

Briatore has not returned to the sport in an official capacity, but is now "executive advisor" with Alpine, while Symonds became the Chief Technical Officer of Formula 1 in 2017. Alonso claimed he did not know about the dodgy plan and kept his victory.

A BAD EXCUSE

September 28 2008, Marina Bay (Singapore)

Mark Webber was running in a strong sixth place in the inaugural and infamous Singapore Grand Prix in 2008 (photo) when his Red Bull-Renault selected fifth and seventh gear simultaneously in Turn 13 on lap 28. The Australian retired with a broken gearbox, and Red Bull team principal Christian Horner suggested that a sudden electrical surge caused by Singapore's underground metro, the Mass Rapid Transit (MRT), had knocked the car's electronics out of action. This was refuted by a MRT spokesman: "There is no MRT track beneath Turn 13 – the nearest MRT tunnel is about 200 meters away. In addition, train wheels and running rails are made of metal and they do not generate static electricity during train operations."

WORLD CHAMPION FOR 20 SECONDS

November 2 2008, Interlagos (Brazil)

Before the final race of the 2008 World Championship, the Brazilian Grand Prix at Interlagos, Lewis Hamilton (McLaren-Mercedes -right)) was leading Felipe Massa (Ferrari – left) by seven points. The start was delayed due to heavy rain, and when the race finally got underway, Massa went into the lead while Hamilton had a hard time further back. Light rain began to fall towards the end of the race, and two laps from the finish, it intensified. With Massa on his way to a great win, Hamilton needed to finish fifth or higher to take the title. When Massa crossed the line, Hamilton was sixth and the Ferrari team celebrated Massa as World Champion. But the Brazilian's title lasted for about 20 seconds. In the spray in the final corner of the last lap, Hamilton grabbed fifth place from Timo Glock (Toyota). It was enough for the McLaren driver to clinch the 2007 World Championship. "We almost did everything perfectly," a disappointed Massa sportingly said after the race. "But we need to congratulate Lewis because he did a great championship and he scored more points than us, so he deserved to be World Champion. I know how to win and I know how to lose, and this is another day of my life from which I am going to learn a lot."

WORLD CHAMPION DENIED SUPER LICENSE

November 01 2009,
Yas Marina, Abu Dhabi

A World Champion was denied a Super License for the inaugural Abu Dhabi in 2009. A World Rally champion, that is. Sebastian Loeb, winner of the World Rally Championship nine times in a row between 2004-2012, was sponsored by Red Bull. He had finished second in the Le Mans 24 Hours in 2006 and Red Bull wanted to put him into a Toro Rosso for a one-off Formula 1 appearance in the final round of the 2009 World Championship. He tested a GP2 car in preparation for his Formula 1 debut, but then FIA stepped in: The Frenchman did not qualify for a Super License. Loeb took it well: "There are no regrets because there was no ambition. The only regret I have is that I'd have had fun doing it. It was a fun project. But hey, that's how it is!" he said.

10's

HAMILTON'S CAR IMPOUNDED AFTER WHEEL-SPIN

March 26 2010,
Melbourne (Australia)

McLaren-Mercedes driver Lewis Hamilton was a little too cheeky when he left Albert Park after practice for the 2010 Australian Grand Prix. In his silver Mercedes road car, he accelerated so hard that the car produced smoke from its spinning rear wheels. Local police officers were not impressed and chased after him with blue lights flashing. Hamilton pulled over and was interviewed for about half an hour and he was also routinely breath tested. In the end, he was allowed to walk to his hotel – the Mercedes was taken away on a truck and impounded for 48 hours. “What I did was silly, and I want to apologize for it,” he said after the incident.

HAVE YOU SEEN THE REMOTE CONTROL?

May 15 2010,
Monte Carlo (Monaco)

Qualifying on the narrow streets of Monte Carlo is always hectic and you certainly do not need any unnecessary distractions. Therefore it was not a surprise that Jenson Button reacted quickly in 2010 when he realised that he still had the remote control for the pit garage timing monitors in the cockpit of his McLaren-Mercedes. Just before he started his quick lap, he threw the remote control out of the car in the Rascasse corner. Without the remote control, Button qualified eighth.

WORLD CHAMPION ATTACKED BY GUNMEN

November 6 2010, Sao Paulo (Brazil)

Reigning World Champion Jenson Button had only just left the gates of the Autodromo Interlagos on the evening of the 2010 Brazilian Grand Prix, when the car had to stop at a traffic light on the Avenida Interlagos. With him in the armour-plated Mercedes-Benz C-class were his dad John, his manager Richard Goddard, his trainer Mike Collier and a professional police driver, hired by Button's McLaren-Mercedes team. Several rows behind them in the traffic, four or five men appeared and began to approach the Mercedes from behind. They looked dodgy, and Button saw one of them take a gun out of his pocket while he was walking towards them. When the World Champion pointed this out to the driver, he reacted swiftly. Trained to get out of such situations, he accelerated and forced his way through, ramming six cars in the process. He then took Button and his other passengers safely back to their hotel. It was never clear if the men wanted to kidnap or rob Button. "It was a pretty scary situation," Button told journalists the following morning (photo). "Looking behind, there were two guys with handguns and one guy with what looked like a machine gun. But our driver was a legend – he got us out of trouble."

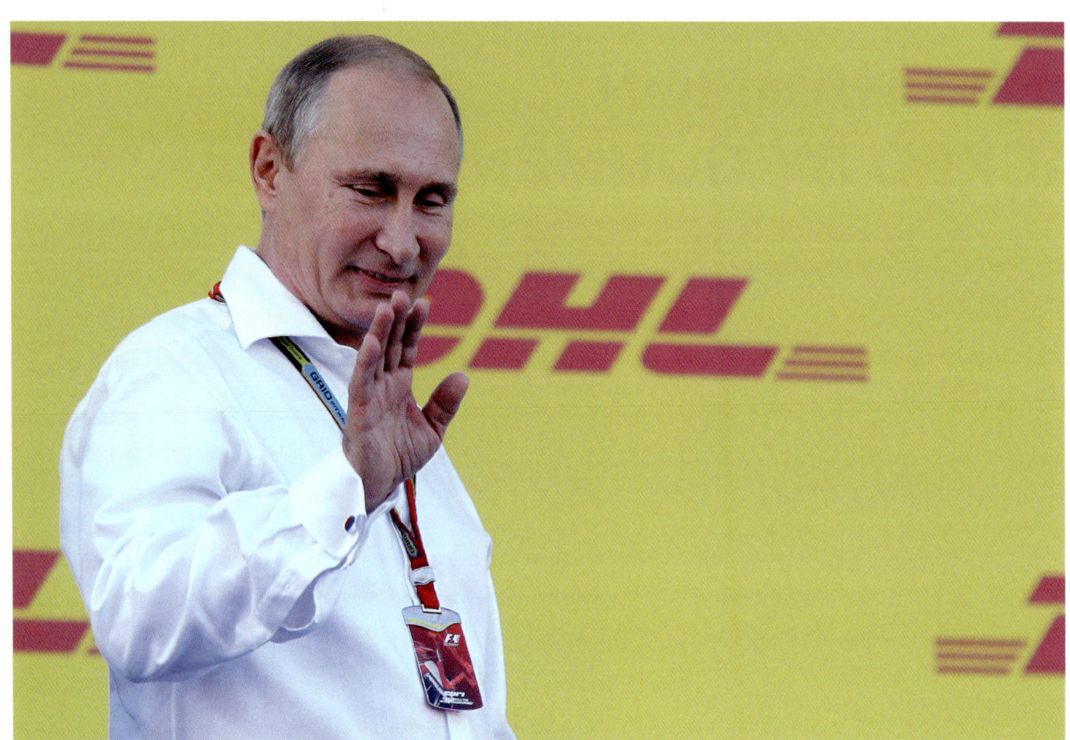

WHEN PUTIN WAS A F1 DRIVER

November 7 2010,
St. Petersburg (Russia)

Russia was important in Formula 1 in 2010. Vitaly Petrov was racing for the Renault team (he was 13th in the World Championship) and in October it was announced that Sochi would host the Russian Grand Prix from 2014 onwards. And then Russian president Vladimir Putin became a F1 driver. At the time, Putin was cultivating his image of an 'action man'. Over the years, he had been seen flipping opponents on the judo mat, riding a horse bare-chested through the mountains and swimming in a Siberian river. Now it was time to test a Renault Formula 1 car, and wearing Renault overalls, he climbed into the car and then drove off by himself along an empty road near St. Petersburg. It was reported that at one point he almost spun but - of course - regained control. The Russian president's F1 debut was later televised on national TV. The Russian Grand Prix remained in the F1 calendar from 2014 to 2021, but is not likely to return any time soon.

PENALIZED BEFORE, DURING AND AFTER THE RACE

May 29 2011,
Monte Carlo (Monaco)

The 2011 Monaco Grand Prix is a race Lewis Hamilton would like to forget. Before the start, the McLaren-Mercedes driver had his best Q3 time deleted for cutting the chicane (photo), and in the race, he got a drive-through penalty for causing an accident with Felipe Massa. And just to finish off a miserable weekend, after the race Hamilton was given a 20-second penalty for causing a collision with Pastor Maldonado a few laps from the end.

LONGEST RACE ALSO THE SLOWEST

June 12 2011, Montreal (Canada)

The 2011 Canadian Grand Prix at the Circuit Gilles Villeneuve in Montreal officially ran for longer than any other round of the FIA Formula 1 World Championship. Rain meant the race began behind a Safety Car, which returned to the pits after five laps. It was back on the circuit only a couple of laps later, when McLaren team-mates Lewis Hamilton and Jenson Button collided on the start/finish straight. The field was released five laps later – but only for six laps.

The intensity of the rain increased, and the Safety Car was deployed a third time. After 24 laps the conditions were so bad that the race was suspended – but without stopping the clock. The field was stationary on the grid while the clock ticked away (photo), and when the race was finally restarted – behind the Safety Car again – it was already after the usual two hour maximum time.

When the chequered flag finally came out – after another two Safety Car deployments – winner Jenson Button's official race time was four hours, four minutes and 39 seconds, making it the longest ever Grand Prix. His McLaren-Mercedes had been stationary for almost half of the 'race time' – which also explains why his average speed of 74.864 km/h is the lowest ever in the history of the FIA Formula 1 World Championship. The slowest average speed for a non-stop race is the 98,17 km/h of Juan-Manuel Fangio in the 1950 Monaco Grand Prix – closely followed by the 100,78 km/h of Alain Prost in the wet 1984 Monaco Grand Prix. The longest uninterrupted race was the 1954 German Grand Prix at the Nürburgring, which Juan-Manuel Fangio (Mercedes) won after three hours, 45 minutes and 46 seconds. For 2012, a four-hour time limit was imposed (with the two-hour limit for races that are not suspended still in force).

WORLD CHAMPIONS EVERYWHERE

March 18 2012,
Albert Park (Australia)

History was made when the 2012 season kicked off with the Australian Grand Prix in Melbourne's Albert Park. For the first time ever in a Grand Prix, there were six World Champions on the grid: Reigning World Champion Sebastian Vettel was joined by Michael Schumacher (1994-1995, 2000-2004 World Champion) Fernando Alonso (2005-2006), Lewis Hamilton (2008), Jenson Button (2009) and 2007 World Champion Kimi Raikkonen, who was making his comeback to F1 after two years in the World Rally Championship.

JUSTICE OR COINCIDENCE?

September 2 2012, Spa-Francorchamps (Belgium)

Romain Grosjean was considered something of a 'wild man' in the summer of 2012. The Lotus-Renault driver was fast, but he was also involved in several incidents. Then came the Belgian Grand Prix. After an aggressive start, Grosjean caused a multiple shunt (photo), which eliminated Lewis Hamilton (McLaren-Mercedes), Sergio Perez (Sauber-Ferrari) and Fernando Alonso (Ferrari). Grosjean was suspended from the next race, the Italian Grand Prix. And who finished on the podium in Monza? Hamilton, Perez and Alonso!

WORLD CHAMPIONS' COINCIDENCES

November 25 2012, Interlagos (Brazil):

When Jenson Button won Michael Schumacher's last race (photo), the 2012 Brazilian Grand Prix, the two World Champions' careers came 'full circle' – the German had won Button's first race, the 2002 Australian Grand Prix. But there are other similar coincidences: Alan Jones won Alain Prost's first Grand Prix (Argentina 1980) – Prost won Jones's last Grand Prix (Australia 1986). Ayrton Senna won Michael Schumacher's first Grand Prix (Belgium 1991) – Schumacher won Senna's last Grand Prix (San Marino 1994). And Alain Prost won Ayrton Senna's first Grand Prix (Brazil 1984) – Senna won Prost's last Grand Prix (Australia 1993).

UNLUCKY NUMBER

March 16 2014,
Albert Park (Australia)

The FIA had always avoided number 13 when distributing starting numbers to the F1 teams, but when the drivers were allowed to choose their own numbers for the 2014 season, Lotus driver Pastor Maldonado promptly picked the unlucky number. “It has a long history in Venezuelan sport,” he explained. Number 13 had only been used once before in the history of the Formula 1 World Championship. Local hero Moises Solana had no issues with 13, and his Centro Sud-BRM carried the number, when he made his F1 debut in the 1963 Mexican Grand Prix. He was classified 11th, despite stopping when his engine expired eight laps from the end. Solana was killed in a hillclimb in Mexico a few years later. In 1976 Great Britain's Divina Galica had number 13 on her privately-entered Surtees for the British Grand Prix, but it didn't bring her any luck as she failed to qualify. With number 13's history, Maldonado's choice for 2014 was a brave one. And perhaps not the best one: The Venezuelan had several incidents during the season and only scored two points.

INSOLVENCY PRACTITIONER AND TEAM PRINCIPAL

November 21 2014,
Yas Marina (Abu Dhabi)

After a difficult 2014-season, the Caterham team entered administration in October and did not go to the United Stated and Brazilian Grands Prix. To find a buyer and keep the team alive, the administrators resorted to crowdfunding, and managed to find the budget – close to $3 million - to attend the final round of the 2014 World Championship, the Abu Dhabi Grand Prix. Chartered accountant and insolvency practitioner Finbarr O'Connell led the administration team, and without any experience in motor racing, he became the Caterham Team Principal in Abu Dhabi. O'Connell duties included the official FIA press conference with Toto Wolff (Mercedes), Christian Horner (Red Bull), Marco Mattiaci (Ferrari), Otmar Szafnauer (Force India) and Claire Williams (Williams). From the pit wall, he watched his drivers Kamui Kobayashi retire from the race on lap 43 and Will Stevens finish in 17th and last place. And that was the end of the insolvency practioner's spell as F1 Team Principal:
No buyer was found and the team's cars, parts equipment and the H.Q. was sold by auction in March 2015.

50 POINTS FOR A SINGLE WIN

November 23 2014, Yas Marina (Abu Dhabi)

When the Formula 1 World Championship started in 1950, a race winner scored eight points. This was increased to nine points in 1961, and in 1991 it was changed again, with the first driver across the line getting 10 points. In 2010 the point system had a major overhaul – since then, the winner is awarded 25 points - with one exception. To spice the championship up and create added interest for the final round, the top-10 finishers in the 2014 Abu Dhabi Grand Prix were awarded double points. Lewis Hamilton won the race (and the World Championship – photo) and is the only driver in the history of Formula 1 who have earned 50 points from a single race. The 'double point' idea was never popular with drivers or fans and was quietly forgotten.

BULL IN CAMOUFLAGE

February 1 2015, Jerez (Spain)

When Red Bull presented their new RB11 at the first 2015 pre-season test in Jerez, the livery was a striking "dazzle" camouflage mixture of black and white stripes, a concept first used by the British and US Navy in the First World War to help conceal the size, distance and heading of ships. For Red Bull it was a question of being different – and of keeping their aerodynamic details secret from their rivals for as long as possible.

"It makes it quite difficult to get detailed photographs of the car at a time of year when we're all trying to be as secretive as we possibly can," team principal Christian Horner explained.

BROKEN NOSE AND BROKEN DREAMS

April 9 2015, Shanghai (China)

Kevin Magnussen seemed destined for great things when he finished second for McLaren in his very first Grand Prix in Australia 2014. Still, when McLaren hired Fernando Alonso for 2015, the young Dane had to vacate his seat and he spent the year as the team's reserve driver. It was a frustrating time, and Magnussen frequently had to let off some steam. When in Shanghai – on duty as McLaren's official reserve driver for the Chinese Grand Prix – he enjoyed the local nightlife a little too much and woke up in his hotel room the following morning with a broken nose - after a bar fight. A few months later, his McLaren contract was not renewed.

A 70-PLACE GRID PENALTY

November 1 2015,
Mexico City (Mexico)

Honda-McLaren had a miserable 2015 season. The new Honda engine was both unreliable and underpowered, and drivers Fernando Alonso and Jenson Button both received several grid penalties for exceeding the allowed allocation of power unit components during the season. In Mexico, Button had several changes to the power unit as well as an unscheduled gearbox change. The result: a combined grid penalty of 70 places!

A ICEMAN CAN WIN WITH EVERYTHING

October 21 2018,
Circuit of the Americas (United States)

Kimi Raikkonen wrote history when he crossed the line to win the 2018 United States Grand Prix on the Circuit of the Americas. At 39 years and 4 days, he almost broke into the top 10 of the Oldest Grand Prix Winners (1981 Belgian Grand Prix winner Carlos Reutemann in 10th place beats him by one day). But more significantly, The Iceman became the only driver in F1 history to have won races with V10, V8 and V6 engines. Raikkonen's first win came in the 2003 Malaysian Grand Prix behind the wheel of a McLaren powered by a Mercedes V10 engine. He went on to win another eight Grands Prix in the V10 era before 2.4-litre V8s had to be used from 2006 onwards. Raikkonen won the 2007 World Championship and a total of 11 Grands Prix for Ferrari and Lotus-Renault with V8 engines. Formula 1 moved to 1.6-litre V6 turbo engines in 2014, and Raikkonen took his historical V6 win in the 2018 United States Grand Prix.

ONE CAR, TWO NUMBERS

November 23 2018, Yas Marina (Abu Dhabi)

From 2014, the drivers had to pick a 'personal' number for their car to carry for the rest of their Formula 1 career, although number 1 is always reserved for the reigning World Champion, but it's optional - if the champion prefers to continue with his usual number, he may do so. The 2013 World Champion Sebastian Vettel (Red Bull) carried number 1 in 2014, but when Lewis Hamilton (Mercedes) won the 2014-2015 titles, he preferred to keep his personal number 44.

The 2016 World Champion Nico Rosberg (Mercedes) retired after the season, so number 1 was also not used in 2017. Hamilton won the title in 2017 but continued with number 44, but when he had clinched the 2018 World Championship, he asked for a special one-off permission to run with number 1 on his car. That's why Lewis Hamilton's Mercedes carried number 1 as well as his usual number 44 in the opening FP1 session before the 2018 Abu Grand Prix. "I thought it would be cool to have it on the car for just one session – so the team have a picture they can really be proud of with number one," Hamilton explained. For FP2 and the rest of the Abu Dhabi weekend, Hamilton ran only with his usual number 44.

WE'VE STARTED – SO LET'S FINISH

November 25 2018, Yas Marina (Abu Dhabi)

The end of the 2018 season in Abu Dhabi was a historical moment. For the first time ever, the same drivers who took part in the opening round of the World Championship, also finished the season. No drivers were replaced during the season, a first for the FIA Formula 1 World Championship. Still, there was a change on the entry list during 2018: the team that started the season in Australia under the name 'Sahara Force India F1 Team', finished the season as 'Racing Point Force India F1 Team' following a buy-out during the summer-break.

1000 RACES – BUT 1003 WINNERS

April 14 2019, Shanghai (China)

The 2019 Chinese Grand Prix was officially the 1000th Grand Prix since the Formula 1 World Championship began in May 1950. Lewis Hamilton won the race at the Shanghai International Circuit, and thus became the 1003rd Grand Prix winner in F1 history. How come? Three Grands Prix actually had two winners: In the 1951 French Grand Prix, Juan Manuel Fangio took over his Alfa Romeo teammate Luigi Faglioli's car after 20 laps, and the drivers shared the 8 points for the win. In the 1956 Argentine Grand Prix, Fangio – now driving for Ferrari - took over teammate Luigi Musso's car after 30 laps (photo), and again the two drivers shared the win (and the 8 points). The 1957 British Grand Prix in Aintree saw Stirling Moss and Tony Brooks share the winning Vanwall (and the 8 points). Coincidentally, their 'shared' wins were also Faglioli's, Musso's and Brooks's first wins - and in the case of Faglioli and Musso their only wins.

A LAUDA 1-2

May 26 2019,
Monte Carlo (Monaco)

Niki Lauda died a few days before the 2019 Monte Carlo Grand Prix. The great Austrian won the World Championship in 1975 and 77 for Ferrari and in 1984 for McLaren. After retiring in 1985, Lauda was a consultant for the Ferrari management, then team principal for Jaguar's F1 team and then part owner and chairman in the Mercedes team. When the Monaco Grand Prix started six days after his death in May 2019, both Lewis Hamilton (Mercedes – left) and Sebastian Vettel (Ferrari – right)) honoured Lauda with special helmets in his colours. Appropriately, they finished first and second.

20's

ONE CIRCUIT, FOUR GRANDS PRIX

October 11 2020, Nürburgring (Germany)

It is officially named the 'Nürburgring Grand Prix Strecke' but it has actually hosted Grands Prix with four different names. A year after its official opening, the new Nürburgring (next door to the iconic 'Nordschleife') organised the 1985 German Grand Prix. In 2009, 2011 and 2013 the German Grand Prix also took place at the Nürburgring. Hockenheim was the traditional home of the German Grand Prix in the 1990s and 2000s, but with Schumacher fever hitting the country, there was room for another Grand Prix. In 1997-1998 the Nürburgring hosted the Luxembourg Grand Prix and the circuit also hosted the European Grand Prix 12 times until 2007. In 2020 'corona season' Nürburgring made another comeback in the Formula 1 calendar, this time with the Eifel Grand Prix (photo).

THE BUSIEST TIME

July 4 2021,
Red Bull Ring (Austria)

The 10 first rounds of the 2020 Formula 1 World Championship were cancelled due to the COVID-19 pandemic, and the season only kicked off with the Austrian Grand Prix on July 5. A year later, the start of the 2021 Austrian Grand Prix on July 4 underlined how well Formula 1 had done during the pandemic: in exactly 12 months the sport held 26 races – 17 in 2020 and nine in 2021. On average that means a Grand Prix every two weeks – in a year which also included a 15-week winter-break and a winter test in Bahrain. Four of the 26 races had been at the Red Bull Ring (two Austrian Grands Prix and two Styrian Grands Prix – photo).

TOTAL RACE DISTANCE: ONE LAP

August 29 2021,
Spa-Francorchamps (Belgium

The 2021 Belgian Grand Prix was planned to begin at 15.00 and run for 44 laps. Persistent rain meant the start was delayed several times but with dusk approaching, it eventually started at 18.17 behind a Safety Car (photo). Three laps behind the Safety Car were completed before the race was red-flagged.

According to the F1 regulations, the results must be taken two laps before the red flag and the official distance of the race was therefore just one lap. With no overtaking allowed behind the Safety Car, the grid positions determined the result with Max Verstappen (Red Bull-Honda) winning in front of George Russell (Williams-Mercedes) and Lewis Hamilton (Mercedes). This is the shortest race in the history of the Formula 1 World Championship, and as less than 75% of the scheduled race distance was completed, only half points were awarded.

MISSILE STRIKE DURING PRACTICE

March 25 2022, Jeddah (Saudi Arabia)

An Aramco oil depot some 15 kms from the Jeddah Corniche Circuit was attacked by drones and missiles from Yemen's Houthi rebels during the first day of practice for the 2022 Saudi Arabian Grand Prix. There was black smoke from the large fire on the horizon, and the FP2 session was delayed by 15 minutes to allow for an emergency meeting between the Formula 1 CEO Stefano Domenicali, the team principals and the drivers. After the meeting, it was announced that the event would continue as planned. Later that evening it took another meeting lasting almost five hours for the local organisers to convince the drivers that they would be safe for the rest of the weekend. Saturday's practice and qualifying and Sunday's race went ahead without further attacks.

PUBLIC TRANSPORT

October 2 2022, Marina Bay (Singapore)

After brake problems during qualifying, Esteban Ocon started the 2022 Singapore Grand Prix from 17th position. The race was not much better for the Alpine driver, who retired after 26 laps when his engine expired in Turn 13 - the part of the circuit furthest from the pit and paddock. With a long journey to get back to his team, Ocon took an unusual route: A marshal took him to the nearest Singapore Mass Rapid Transit station and Ocon - still wearing his helmet and overalls - went back to the paddock on the metro. He later talked about the reaction from his fellow passengers: “Who is this weirdo - why is he so sweaty?”

OCON TAKES THE PASTOR'S RECORD

July 2 2023,
Red Bull Ring (Austria)

Pastor Maldonado did win the 2012 Spanish Grand Prix in a Williams-Renault but his main claim to fame was a... let's say 'spectacular driving style' which included its fair share of spins, accidents and penalties. In the 2015 Hungarian Grand Prix, the good Pastor earned himself three penalties - one for a collision with Sergio Perez, one for speeding in the pit lane and one for overtaking under the Safety Car. But in the Austrian Grand Prix in 2023, Esteban Ocon almost made Maldonado look like an amateur.

The Alpine-Renault driver had a five-second penalty for an unsafe release during a pit stop and no fewer than four penalties for 'track limit violations'. Five penalties in one race was a new record for Ocon!

WINNING AT HOME – DESPITE SIX PIT-STOPS

*August 27 2023,
Zandvoort (Holland)*

Max Verstappen (Red Bull-Honda) broke or equalled a lot of records with his dominant 2023 season. One of the more unusual ones came in his home race, the Dutch Grand Prix in Zandvoort. In ever-changing conditions, he made six pit-stops but still managed to win the race. The only other driver to win a Grand Prix after six pit-stops is Jenson Button (McLaren-Mercedes) in the dramatic 2011 Canadian Grand Prix.

CAREFUL WITH THE INSURANCE

December 8 2024,
Yas Marina (Abu Dhabi)

After Pierre Gasly finished the 2024 finale in Abu Dhabi in seventh place, several news outlets reported that the Frenchman had made F1 history: It was said that Gasly had cost the Alpine team absolutely nothing in crash damage over the season. It was a nice story and Gasly went along with it. “It makes it easier to insure my cars back home,” he joked. A closer look at Gasly's 2024 season reveals a slightly different picture – his Alpine did sustain damage in a couple of races. The contact with teammate Esteban Ocon on the first lap in Monaco forced him to change the rear wing and another crash with Ocon in Japan damaged the floor of his car. Gasly may argue that none of these incidents were his fault, but they did affect the team's budget. But two minor incidents in the longest season in F1 history are still impressive.

The Alternative F1 History

Text: Peter Nygaard
Photos: Peter Nygaard
Editor: Jesper Helmin
Layout: Pallas Group

ISBN: 9788794190367
1. edition, 1. circulation
Printed at GPS Group, 2025

Helmin & Sorgenfri
Nivå Strandpark 21
DK-2990 Nivå
Denmark

www.helminsorgenfri.dk